SEPARATION ANXIETY

SEPARATION

MIJI CAMPBELL

ANXIETY

A COMING OF middle AGE STORY

*to Sheila,
Enjoy the
journey!
Miji
Campbell*

Writinerant PRESS

Writinerant Press
22 Abraham Close
Red Deer, Alberta T4R 3A9
www.writinerant.com

Catalogue data available from Library and Archives Canada
ISBN 978-0-9938032-0-8 (pbk.)
ISBN 978-0-9938032-1-5 (ebook)

The author acknowledges the support of the Province of Alberta
through the Alberta Foundation for the Arts.

The names of some people and places have been
changed to preserve privacy.

Cover and text design by Jennifer Griffiths
Copy editing by Michelle MacAleese
Cover illustration courtesy of Megan Raley
Photographs by Jennifer Griffiths
Family photos courtesy of Miji Campbell
Kingsland map © Bekins Moving and Storage (Canada) Ltd.
The book introduced on page 166 is *The Anxiety & Phobia Workbook,
3rd Edition*, by Edmund J. Bourne
Printed and bound in Canada by Marquis

12 13 14 15 16   5 4 3 2 1

For my mother and father

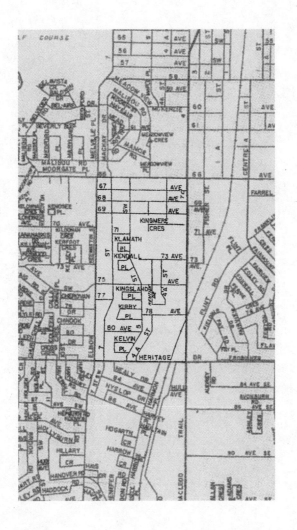

THREE MONTHS BEFORE I was born, my mother was putting bed linens away in the back bedroom closet. Standing tiptoe on a little wooden stool, she stretched her pregnant five-foot frame just far enough to stack the sheets—freshly plucked from the clothesline and folded smooth—into neat rows on the highest shelf. Suddenly, the stool tipped, sliding out from under her, and skittered across the hardwood. My mother fell, twisting to avoid landing baby-side-down, wrenching her knee, ripping ligaments as she hit the floor.

It would be days before she agreed to see a doctor, who encased her leg in a plaster cast from waist to ankle. My mother spent the rest of her pregnancy hobbling on a single crutch, worrying about this baby that seldom moved.

On the day I was born, the nurse had to ask the doctor what to do first: birth the baby or remove the cast. They cut the cast away and I arrived shortly after. The left side of my face had been flattened by three months of imposed stillness. My mother waited for leg surgery that would leave a white scar in the shape of a cross on her knee.

This became the working model for our relationship: my mother would protect me from all bumps and falls, with considerable contortion, pain and self-sacrifice, and I would never, really, leave the womb.

PART 1

{ **ONE** }

THE UNDERGROUND PARKADE is silent, dimly lit, filled with nighttime suspense. Footsteps echo as I run to my car, parked in shadows beneath heating ducts and air exchangers that suddenly cycle on with a giant mechanical moan. I fumble my keys into the lock, slide into the front seat and lock the door. Push in the clutch. Start the engine. First gear whines up the steep exit ramp where the garage door lifts, mercifully, on clicking chains. In darkness pierced by headlights and streetlights, I drive the twenty blocks home to Kingsland.

Sanctuary.

One month earlier, I had moved out. Officially. My two older sisters had left home in their turn and now it was my time to go. I was twenty-four years old.

It was 1984, a portentous year to be teaching English at the Calgary high school I'd attended six years earlier. The plan was to stay at my parents' house just long enough to get my student loans under control and save a little money. My "hope chest" was piled in the back bedroom closet: a cache of new dishes, bed and bath linens, kitchen gadgets and small appliances. A Picasso print, *Le Bouquet*, was rolled up in a cardboard tube.

When I saw the apartment I knew it was the place for me. A three-floor walk-up with underground parking. Close enough to work and the neighbourhood I grew up in without being in the neighbourhood. This is independence, I thought, as I signed my cheques for the damage deposit and first month's rent. As I moved all my stuff in over the Christmas break, I was happy. I'd been dreaming of my first apartment since I was ten.

I hung Picasso above my bed. I arranged my weightier books from university on new IKEA bookshelves. I stacked pale peach towels in the linen closet and filled my spice rack with cumin, coriander and Hungarian paprika. I could pick up pâté and croissants from Woodward's Famous Food Floor on my way home from work—just like a young, single career woman would.

I was going to love this life.

That first night in the apartment, I snuggled under my new flowered Marimekko sheets and waited for my first sleep as an independent adult. Turned from one side to the other. Flipped my pillow to its cool underside. Took a sip of water. Glanced at the clock.

Restlessness nudged into worry.

Why couldn't I fall asleep?

The next night, same thing. And the night after that.

◇ ◇ ◇

2:35

A red dot in the lower-left corner of the display indicates "a.m." The dot in the upper-right reminds me that, in just four hours, the alarm will wake me up. That is, if I ever get to sleep in the first place.

I consider my options. I could roll over for the hundredth time. Flip the pillow. Fluff the duvet. I could get up and flick on the TV, where, I have discovered, there are commercials that ask "Why aren't you sleeping? You'll feel terrible in the morning."

The familiar anxiousness begins. Hot prickles reach across my scalp and down my forehead and cheeks. Breath comes in quick, shallow scoops. Heart races in my chest and pounds in my ears. Stomach lurches in a sudden wave of fear.

I am wide awake.

After a string of sleepless nights, I casually mentioned my problem to some of the teachers at work. They gave stock soporific remedies: hot bath, warm milk, good book. Some suggested sex or—since I was unattached at the time— masturbation. One friend told me about a jag of insomnia during her marriage breakup. She had no advice but was sympathetic. Finally, I confessed to my mother.

"Just come home to sleep," she said.

It was a strange double life. Each night, I'd give sleep the old college try. (I'd gone away to university, after all, and had slept just fine.) After a couple hours of trying, I'd get up, throw on my grey sweats and drive home. I'd unlock the back door—Mom and Dad had long since gone to bed— tiptoe down the hallway, crawl into my single bed and fall instantly asleep. Each morning, I'd rush back to my apartment to shower, get dressed and go to work.

My father, noting this late-night trend, was mystified by my boomerang home. He'd left his own parents when he was eighteen and never looked back. "What are you afraid of? Bears?" he asked in that same sonorous, derisive tone he used to dissect the mysteries of my mother's allegiance to the Catholic Church.

I tried to explain that I really wasn't afraid of anything, I just couldn't get to sleep.

"Maybe you can get day rates at your apartment."

I could forgive myself the problems I'd had as a child sleeping at Brownie camp or my failed attempts to sleep over at my best friend Karen's. (Her dad had to bundle me in a blanket and carry me back to my porch at dusk.) But there was an implacable, arms-crossed, foot-tapping side to me that didn't like these adult sleepovers at my parents' and wanted to get past it. Now.

So, every two or three nights, I'd make myself stay in my apartment. Hot bath. Warm milk. Good book. I'd agree to give myself one hour to fall gently asleep. At the end of my deadline, wide awake, I would feel the frustration. "Why can't I do this? What's wrong with me?" Then the panic. "I'll be so tired tomorrow I won't be able to teach." Most nights, I gave up before it got too ridiculously late, and drove home.

It was clear this not-sleeping thing was *not* going to pass. I went to our family doctor. He gave me sleeping pills, Halcion, for ten days to break the cycle. I got a few nights' solid sleep. When the prescription was done, sleeplessness returned. "Maybe you need a roommate," the doctor suggested. "Maybe a pet bird."

Maybe my problem needed younger guns.

I went to see a brand new doctor—a woman. With her long ginger hair and crisp white coat, royal blue stethoscope looped around her neck, she seemed the model of progressive medical practice. I told her about my insomnia issues. She took my blood pressure, listened to my lungs, peered in my ears and down my throat and assured me that everything looked fine, physically. She asked about family, relationships, work in general.

"Have you always wanted to be a teacher?"

That was a tricky one to answer. I'd always wanted to be a writer, but that sounded flaky. In any case, I should have been discovered by now as a promising young novelist or poet, apprenticing under some famous writer's wing in graduate school. I knew I wanted to write, but I didn't know what.

After I finished my English degree, I spent some time kicking the career tires in marketing and public relations. I toured a local PR firm. The vice-president, his fingers and wrists loaded with gold, suggested I learn how to type.

Teaching became my reasonable, responsible career choice. The writing dream was shelved along with my Norton anthologies of English literature.

"Are you enjoying your job?" the doctor asked.

"Absolutely! It's great. I'm teaching at the high school I went to—just like *Welcome Back, Kotter*! It's fun, but busy. The first year can be a little intense."

She nodded and smiled. Then she launched into a little lecture about personality types. Type A's are ambitious, goal-oriented, competitive and self-critical. Type B's are relaxed, non-competitive and tend to go with the flow.

"Would you say that you're more of a Type A?"

"I guess," I answered hesitantly. Where was she going with this?

"I'm wondering if you might be depressed."

Depressed? What did she mean by that? Depressed was Charlie Brown talking to Linus in the Saturday comics. A person might say "I'm depressed" after a tough week, a sad breakup, a bad haircut. I didn't know anyone who was depressed all the time. That kind of depressed was for people with horrible hardships or sad childhoods.

"I'm not depressed. I just can't sleep in my apartment."

Patiently, the doctor explained how the ketones (or something) in my brain had been depleted from lack of sleep, which, over time, could lead to depression. She prescribed Anafranil, an antidepressant that would restore my brain chemical balance. Dutifully, without question ("Will this help me sleep tonight?") I took the prescription and drove straight to the Kingsland drugstore. The plastic vial was tagged with stickers about alcohol, drowsiness and heavy machinery. The pharmacist dispensed even more warnings, which I missed in my rush to get out of the store. To appear normal.

I took one tiny white pill that night. Still no sleep. I didn't go to work the next day because I felt spaced-out on top of the usual tiredness. I couldn't even nap. I called the doctor. She increased the dosage.

Afraid of what might happen (in a *Go Ask Alice* sense), I went back to my parents' house to be "sick" waiting for the Anafranil to work.

Each morning, my mother encouraged me to go to school.

I said I was scared to drive.

She suggested I walk. "The fresh morning air will wake you up."

Somehow, I knew that showing up in that state—stoned, cold, exhausted—would cause my teaching confidence to crumble as well.

Mom didn't like the way our private pact around not sleeping was beginning to compromise my day job. Insomnia could be beaten, she believed, if you denied that it was even a problem. This approach had kept her from sleeping soundly for years.

My mother was a teacher, too. At eighteen, she began her career in a one-room schoolhouse in Allan, Saskatchewan. On her first day of work, the story goes, she had to hitch up a team of horses and drive a wagonload of children to school.

By the end of the week, she had to strap her oldest student, who was one year younger and one foot taller than her.

It was this story that inspired me to get past my own fears and out the door for my first day of teaching a few months earlier. When it came to teaching, Mom gave excellent advice. When it came to sleeping, she didn't.

Don't let yourself get overtired.

I was seriously overtired. But this wide-awake fuzzy-edged world of Anafranil scared me more than not sleeping. I couldn't wait three weeks to get to the other side of "mood improvement" if it meant wandering, zombie-like, through every day. I felt like some tragic character from a Greek myth—the one that asks for eternal life but forgets to ask for eternal youth. I'd asked for sleep but forgotten to ask them to let me close my eyes and lie down.

I flushed the Anafranil down the toilet. I was not depressed. I did not need antidepressants. There was nothing wrong with my brain.

I took a multivitamin instead.

After five consecutive sick-leave days—more than my mother took in her entire teaching career—I went back to work. The first objective in my daily plan book read: "Students will be able to recognize their teacher."

I poured all my energy into teaching. I performed shows daily in front of every class, jumped through the hoops of evaluation with perfectly planned lessons and juggled the roles of confident new teacher (with great clothes and many shoes), extracurricular booster (helping with the spring drama production and attending more basketball games

than I ever had in high school) and young but capable colleague (joking in the smoke-filled staffroom with teachers
who had taught me just a few years before).

Nightly, after the crowds had gone home, I would return
to my beloved apartment, make supper and plan my lessons
for the next day. Macbeth's grief over his own lost sleep had
never seemed so poignant. *"Sleep that knits up the ravell'd
sleave of care…"*

What had I done to murder my sleep?

Bedtime. Time for my private high-wire act. I would
stand on the platform, close my eyes and try to remember
everything I'd forgotten about falling asleep. I would imagine myself waking up to morning—hours of gentle sleep
behind me—and step out on the wire. Within a few brave
steps, I would falter, lose my balance and fall to the net
below.

Just come home to sleep.

◊ ◊ ◊

AT EASTER BREAK in April, I flew to Vancouver to visit a
girlfriend. Her West End apartment, close to the edgy Davie
Street and the night hum of English Bay, was a world apart
from the safe predictability of my neighbourhood in Calgary. I spent my days shopping relentlessly. Clothes. Shoes.
Accessories. West 4th. Broadway. Granville. At night, I slept.
On two square foam cushions shoved together on the hardwood floor, I slept. While Ruth and her boyfriend argued
and thrashed and smoked in the bedroom beside me, I slept.

Later that week, while shopping at the Pacific Centre, I ran into my mother, who was also on holiday in Vancouver with a friend. I could have cried. There I was, looking like an adult, and there she was to catch me out. "How's the sleeping?" she asked. I could have lain on the floor of Eaton's ladies wear and kicked and pounded and screamed.

With adult politeness, Ruth suggested my mother and her friend join us for lunch at a bistro called Le Crocodile. I couldn't look at Mom or have a conversation with her. I let Ruth carry on with her big voice and gestures. I could feel Mom's eyes on my face. Wanting me to look at her. Insisting. No. I looked at the menu. The traffic outside. The posters on the wall. Anywhere but those brown eyes so different from my own. Deep pools of sympathy and gentle admonishment. In her eyes, I would see that I was just a kid after all, play-acting in the big city. Dressing up. Putting on high heels and glamorous hats and gloves and going out to luncheons. It would be bedtime soon and Mommy would be calling. Don't look.

I returned to Calgary, my apartment and insomnia.

By the long weekend in May, I resolved to quit this pattern of going home to sleep once and for all. I just wasn't trying hard enough. Friday night, I made myself stay in my apartment. No sleep. Saturday night. No sleep. Sunday. Try harder.

It is now eleven o'clock. A reasonable adult bedtime.

I turn out the light and lie down on my bed. Think about the day's events. Think about the week ahead.

I look at the clock.

One hour gone.

Maybe I should try praying. I make a quick sign of the cross. An old charm for good luck—a furtive ritual before exams.

"Hail Mary, full of Grace. The Lord is with thee. Blessed art thou amongst women and blessed is the fruit of thy womb, Jesus."

I never understood that "fruit of thy womb" line as a kid.

Maybe I should pray out loud.

"Holy Mary, Mother of God, pray for us sinners."

These prayers are so *sibilant*.

"Forgive us our trespasses. As we forgive those who trespass against us…"

The snakelike hiss of sin.

I should be taking this more seriously. Be praying on my knees.

I stretch one leg down to the floor, throw off my duvet and feel the chill of a dark new morning. I slither out and kneel beside the bed, martyr-like, forehead resting on my prayer-clasped hands.

Is there a patron saint for sleeping?

I look at the clock.

Two hours gone.

I move to the living room and stretch out on the floor.

The carpet is rough against my skin.

Just relax. Take a deep breath.

I feel tears gather and catch in my throat.

Why can't I sleep? What am I doing wrong?

I start to cry, hitting the carpet with my fist.

It is morning.

I hear birds chirping and the familiar sound of the trees rustling outside the bedroom window. By the angle of the sun through the curtains, I know that I have slept later than I wanted to. There are sounds and smells from the kitchen. Toast popping, cutlery clanking. My dad is making his lunch. I'm too embarrassed to face him. To interrupt his routine.

I lie in bed, wondering what May long weekends for normal adults feel like. Camping. Hiking. Partying.

I see the doorknob turn slowly, quietly. Soon Mom will peer around the edge of the door to see if I'm awake. Just as she did when I took my afternoon naps. Should I pretend that I'm asleep? She tiptoes across the room and bends over me. "Why can't I sleep?" I ask her. "What am I doing wrong?" Hot tears of shame. "I'm no good at anything."

Mom murmurs and tries to pet me. I throw off her hand. I kick against the covers. "I'm stupid. I can't do anything right." I lift my head and slam it down on the pillow. I snarl through clenched teeth, "I'm going crazy." I grab chunks of my hair and pull.

My mother rushes into the hallway. I hear her dial the phone. She talks in urgent whispers to Dr. Mahoney's answering service. I sit up and stare at the wad of hair in my hand. Somewhere inside me, a calm voice reassures.

You know you're not crazy.

△ △ △

I'M SITTING IN MY CAR in front of a three-storey character home just off 17th Avenue. This is the address I've been given. It is a warm, blue-sky afternoon, the trees leafed out in the first green of June. I have rushed from school to get here on time. I am wearing a new white cotton suit with a red-and-white-striped polo shirt. I want to look self-assured. Confident. Pulled together even though I may be falling apart.

I walk up the steps to the porch. A handwritten card points up the stairs. I climb two flights to a small attic room. A room like I used to imagine where they kept that lady on our street who went crazy. Like Rochester's wife in *Jane Eyre*. But this room is filled with sunlight and gentle breezes.

This is my first visit to a psychologist.

I try hard to sound like I don't need one. I speak quickly, using bigger words than usual. My life sounds perfectly normal when I lay it out like this. Great job, excellent parents, nice friends, new apartment. A bit of a sleeping problem.

She wants to know more about this. So I fill her in. Shove my night fears under this rational daylight. Condense six months of frustration and shame into a comic monologue: "So there I am, past midnight, pajamas tucked into my sweatpants, speeding down Elbow Drive in my green Renault Le Car, to sneak into my parents' house."

The psychologist looks thoughtful and asks a few more questions. "How would you describe your relationship with your parents?"

"My mom and I are really close. We're a lot alike. Everyone says so. We like talking, meeting new people, teaching.

We love to shop together—especially at Chinook Centre."

I pause. I know she is waiting for the rest of the answer.

"I've never been close to my dad."

She nods and makes a few notes.

"Has moving into your own apartment made you feel homesick?"

"No. I wanted to move out on my own. I'd been stockpiling housewares for months!"

"But you've never been able to sleep in your apartment?"

"No."

Exposed, embarrassed, I decide to tell her.

"I've always had trouble sleeping away from home. Even when my mom went out for the evening, I wouldn't be able to sleep until she came home and kissed me good night. But that was when I was just a kid."

Suddenly, I'm remembering a school trip to Ottawa when I was seventeen. I didn't sleep for the entire week, my stomach in knots. I'd had lofty plans to go to Carleton University for journalism but decided, after that experience, to stay close to home in Calgary. Four years later, I moved away to university in Edmonton. Even then, I had trouble sleeping because my roommate snored. I'd phone my mom every Sunday night in tears. My roommate offered to sleep in the living room.

I'd forgotten that until this moment.

"Am I ever going to be able to sleep in my apartment?"

The psychologist doesn't answer right away. She shows me some breathing and relaxation techniques. I lie on the floor to practise.

She wants to see me again in a week. I swallow my disappointment. She hasn't cured me.

"No problem."

She gives one firm directive as I leave: "Do not go back to your mother's house to sleep."

That night, I go out with friends, drink wine and make jokes about having to go to bed all by myself. I get back to my apartment around midnight. Unlocking the door, I step into the dark hallway. I feel the familiar tightness in my chest, the choking sensation in my throat, tears burning in eyes squeezed shut. Every part of my body aches to turn around and go home. I lean against the door, sobbing.

I have never felt so alone.

◇ ◇ ◇

It is nighttime in my bedroom and I am afraid.
I am afraid of the dark behind the closet.
I am afraid of being the last one to fall asleep.
I want to call out for my mother,
Who will sit beside me until sleep comes.

◇ ◇ ◇

"IF YOU STILL can't sleep," says the psychologist at our next session, "you might as well use the time productively."

The night shift begins. I set up the ironing board with the laundry basket beside it. I thread a needle and poke it into the arm of the love seat. Ready to sew buttons. Stitch fallen hems. I stack English essays that need to be graded on my dining room table.

I try to sleep for forty-five minutes. No luck. I get up, snap on the light. Do forty push-ups and sit-ups. Scrawl pissed-off thoughts into the journal waiting on my nightstand: "Funny how my circadian rhythms are so fucked up." Sometimes I laugh out loud.

I proceed to chores. Ironing. Sewing. Marking. I hear birds as early morning light slants into my apartment. My head aches. I lie down and drift into a half sleep. Soon it will be time to get up. Go to work.

Two hard weeks go by. I am driving back to my apartment late one night. It is pouring rain and I am crying. Tired of trying to solve this on my own. Tired of being tired.

I turn off Macleod Trail into Kingsland.

Sanctuary.

◊ ◊ ◊

THE HOUSE IS STILL. Rain beats on the roof. I stare at the ceiling as I lie in my childhood bed. My mother sits beside me, yawning, waiting for me to fall asleep.

I remember all the nights we have spent like this.

When I was afraid of the dark behind the closet doors. Afraid of my sister's noisy breathing. Afraid of being the last one to fall asleep.

The rain subsides. I hear the intermittent plunk of raindrops on the eaves.

I am still awake. Wide awake. Irrevocably awake.

I get up and drive home to my apartment, curiously relieved.

◊ ◊ ◊

WHEN I WAS EIGHT, I joined Brownies. Meetings of the 75th Brownie pack were held in St. Augustine School's multi-purpose room every Monday evening. Brownies intrigued me, not for the baggy uniforms and sagging leotards, but for the pure potential of those brown sleeves to be filled with merit badges, each one an embroidered yellow symbol of achievement. My mother once showed me a photo in our community newspaper of a girl who had received every badge, so many, in fact, that she wore a special sash from shoulder to hip to accommodate the extras. This became my goal: to have the most badges in my pack.

The first few were simple—things I did anyway like Book Lover's or Writer's or Minstrel's. Even the Housekeeping badge was easy, once I developed the knack for Bisselling carpets and making Jell-O. Semaphore was more of a challenge, flapping the flags through the alphabet and lifesaving SOS for our pack leader Brown Owl's discerning eye.

It was the Toymaker's badge that nearly destroyed me. The criteria seemed straightforward: make three toys from materials found around the house. I pored over craft books of things to make out of construction paper, wood scraps and plastic bleach bottles. The first toy I made from an empty dish-soap bottle topped with a Styrofoam ball for a head and a steel pot scrubber for hair. I glued on jiggly eyes and folded a checkered dishcloth into an apron. Ta-da! A textbook "Kitchen Kate." My second toy was a puzzle of triangular plywood pieces—an odd choice given my impatience with puzzles generally—and the third, I'd decided, was going to be a really amazing stuffed toy. Mom suggested I start with some old blue leotards, pilled and balled, lying in the bottom of the rag bag. The entire idea repelled me; stuffed toys could only be made of fluffy Orlon in pastel pinks or yellows. Mom showed me how I might cut one leotard leg and stuff it with more rags to fashion a kind of rag doll–teddy thing. It was ugly. I would be the laughing stock of the Brownie pack. "It has to be a good toy," I cried, throwing the blue lump across the kitchen table.

"You're overtired. You're beyond yourself," said my mother, sending me to bed.

The next morning, I woke to a little blue creature perched on my pillow. It had pom-pom arms and legs and a pom-pom toque. Two plastic upholstery tacks were screwed in for eyes and red felt was glued into a wan smile. Three buttons marched down its round tummy. It was kind of cute, like a miniature blue snowman.

I packed up my toy creations for the next Brownie meeting and imagined how that new badge—a Noah's Ark—would look on my sleeve.

I lost the badge just minutes after I received it during our assembly around the Brownie toadstool. Frantic, I checked the multi-purpose room, my dad's car, everywhere I had been since the Brownie meeting ended. For the next week, I prayed to St. Anthony. My dad, noting this losing-things trend, showed me how to make a checklist to take with me from home to school. He recalls that I lost that, too.

My Toymaker's badge was found, eventually, by eagle-eyed Brown Owl. I was relieved and happy, but always felt a twinge of guilt when I looked down my sleeve at the badge, a symbol I would later recognize as more albatross than ark.

◊ ◊ ◊

INSOMNIA PERSISTED through the summer holidays, its jagged edges smoothed by late-night wine and mornings where I knew I could stay in bed, dozing.

"If you still can't sleep," said the psychologist at our next session, "you should increase your physical activity."

I signed up for aerobics and swam laps at the south YMCA, where as a kid I'd spent summer afternoons splashing in the pool and running on the patio, making sloppy wet footprints on the hot cement.

My hope was to get so exhausted that sleep would be inevitable. I was in the best physical shape of my life, but felt dull—lifeless—with dark-circled eyes in my too-pale face, like the doomed somnambulist in Dr. Caligari's sideshow, dreaming of release.

With the first of the back-to-school flyers, I began to worry about my return to classes and routine. If I couldn't sleep then I couldn't teach. On a Sunday night in late August, my oldest sister, Kim, phoned me. This was a rare occurrence. She and I weren't in the habit of calling each other or staying connected in any sense. She lived in another city with a university professor twenty-four years her senior and spent most of her time experimenting with ethnic cooking, reading classics like *Lolita* and—I would later discover—managing the professor's rage.

I knew that Kim had trouble sleeping, too. As a child she'd avoided sleepovers and summer camps and felt that awful rising fear as everyone else fell effortlessly asleep. Like me, she relied on Mom's bedside vigil. Our mother in flannelette pajamas, hair in curlers stabbed with pink plastic pins and trussed in a blue cotton hairnet, moved from room to room over creaking floorboards, giving a benediction for our sleep through a sacrifice of hers.

"I know why you're not sleeping," my sister tells me.

Her words are like water.

{ TWO }

I'D LIVED MY ENTIRE CHILDHOOD in a three-bedroom bungalow in a Calgary suburb called Kingsland. That I was spending a good chunk of my adult life there was an ironic testimony to my father's one guiding principle in raising a family: Never move. Stable home begets stable children.

Mom and Dad had come to parenthood late by 1950s' standards. Both were in their thirties by the time Kim was born in Goose Bay, Labrador, where Dad, an air traffic controller, was stationed in the air force. As a bachelor, he'd enjoyed postings in Toronto, Edmonton and Frobisher Bay, miles away from his happy but commonplace boyhood in Whitewood, Saskatchewan, where his father was the town dentist and his mother a high-minded Methodist. Now a family man himself, Dad worried about the pitfalls of a peripatetic military life.

My mother's goal, vaguely concealed from my dad, was to have four more children.

She'd had a peripatetic life of her own. As a child she'd lived in Winnipeg, Regina and Saskatoon—moves necessitated by a father who had a great head for business but drank. He eventually deserted the family, leaving my grandmother to find work while my mother took care of her younger brother and sister. After high school, my mother attended Normal School in Saskatoon and began her teaching career six weeks later in the one-room schoolhouse in Allan. She went on to teach in Saskatoon; Fort Nelson, British Columbia; and North Bay, Ontario, where she met my dad.

They went looking—along with the rest of their generation—for the proof of 1950s' prosperity: a steady job, a new car, a nice house in a safe neighbourhood.

My father began his sales career with Pyrotenax of Canada within days of his formal military discharge. The personnel manager in Toronto heard his assertive footfall on the stairs and hired him on the spot. Dad would open up the Prairie territory, spreading the good news about Pyrotenax heating cables, an innovative and important technology for the rapidly growing cities of the west. Calgary, population 180,000, would become home.

I was born on the edge of winter in December 1959, the third and last child. Things were pretty much in place when I arrived: father at work and mother at home with my sisters Kim, four, and Robin, one and a half. With her own children, my mother intended to get things right. We would have a golden childhood.

Our U-shaped crescent is called Kirby Place. Tall green streetlights have little doors in the base for short magic creatures. There are stucco houses trimmed in blue, red or brown. Some have carports. Our house is green with cantaloupe-coloured trim. On the front lawn, two slender birch trees are staked with wires to keep them safe from wind. Mugo pines flank the front porch, guarding our castle in the Kingdom of Kingsland.

Inside the front door, the entryway is filled with sunlight. Long hallway rugs run over gleaming hardwood. The living room is mostly for grown-ups. The black chesterfield has silver sparkles and green satin cushions. There is an armchair with scratchy brown stripes where my father reads *The Calgary Herald* after unlacing his shoes and putting his sock feet up on the footstool. Sometimes he lets me squish in beside him. Here is my mother's prized cricket chair, where she does her mending. But the rocking chair is my favourite, its brown and orange cushions stitched with Jack and the Beanstalk figures. A donkey, a little boy, a giant. The rocking chair creaks back and forth, a refuge for my mother and me on those nights when I cry and can't sleep.

There is a coffee table in a shamrock shape. A Hummel figurine stands in the middle. I like this boy who whistles and carries an umbrella and a little suitcase. The *Merry*

Wanderer. Do not touch! There are smaller Hummel figurines on the curio shelf on the wall. Beside the shelf is a
large painting of a woman pouring milk from a jug. A white
cloth covers her hair and I think she is a man.

Our television, a Magnavox, sits against the wall. Every
morning, we are allowed to watch the Friendly Giant
arrange his little chairs. *Here's a chair that rocks and another
that two can curl up in.* On *Romper Room*, I wait for Miss
Ann to look through her magic mirror and see me, standing
so straight and tall with a basket on my head, and say my
name. *I see Laurie and Shirley and Bobby…* In the afternoons,
my mother sets up the ironing board in front of the TV. She
presses my father's hankies from damp rolls she keeps in
the fridge. The smell of hot steam and Glide spray starch,
the hiss of the iron and the opening heartbeat pulse of *People in Conflict* make me sleepy.

The dining room table is round and polished and has
four ladder-back chairs. This table is for company. We
unfold the linen tablecloth from the tall buffet hutch and
carefully set out the good dishes: white china plates with
swirly burgundy edges, polished silverware and crystal wine
glasses that smell of dust.

The kitchen floor is a checkerboard of tomato-red and
celery-green tiles. Copper-bottom pots and pans hang on
the wall covered in brick-patterned wallpaper. We eat most
of our meals at the beige Arborite table on red Melmac plates
set on paper serviettes. Shreddies for breakfast. Cheez Whiz
sandwiches for lunch. Suppers of roast beef or pork chops
or chicken with iceberg lettuce salads drizzled with orange

French dressing. On no-meat Fridays, we sometimes eat sardines. I prefer desserts: yum-yum cake, jam-jam cookies, Whip'n Chill parfaits.

Along the back hallway are three bedrooms. Robin and I share the mint-green room with pink dressers and a lamp with dancing elephants. The blue room with striped wallpaper belongs to Kim alone. There is a single bed with a curving headboard my dad made from copper (Pyrotenax) pipe. A fluffy toy dog named Butch sits on the bed beside a thick maroon book, *Reader's Digest Condensed*. My sister reads constantly in her silent blue room with a yellow bag of Dad's Oatmeal Cookies stashed under the covers.

Mom and Dad have a candy-cane room with a red-and-white-striped bedspread, curtains and laundry hamper. The tall chest of drawers belongs to my father, with loose change, cufflinks and peppermints strewn on top. Socks, pajamas and white shirts with blue cardboard bow ties from the dry cleaner's are stacked in the drawers beneath. The bottom drawer sticks, heavy with photo albums, the kind with black pages and gold photo stickers. I sit on the floor and look at the old photographs, curious about the strangers who stare back. My parents' wedding portrait is tucked away in a brown accordion file. I am startled to see my dad with a thin moustache and wavy dark brown hair. The angular grey brush cut is all I've ever known. I wonder where my mom's wedding dress, an elegant cocktail-length satin, might be now. It's not in the yellow plastic garment bag in their closet. I know. I've snooped. But there is a silky white negligee with pearl buttons.

Mom's dresser has a big mirror with six drawers side by side. One drawer is for hiding birthday presents. Satin slips and flannel pajamas are folded in a middle drawer beside the *Children's Illustrated Bible*—mercifully out of my sight and nighttime imagination. (The pictures terrify me. In one, everyone is bleeding, their hands cut off. There is another picture of an old man, bare-naked, with horrid bumps and sad eyes, leaning on a cane. The scariest picture is the devil, half-man, half-goat, with pointy ears and horns, smiling wickedly as he tempts Jesus on a cliff.)

The top drawer holds an assortment of clip-on earrings, gloves, scarves and a beaded black purse for evening. A small statue of the Virgin Mary stands on the dresser. She smells like sulphur and glows in the dark. Beside her is a golden bottle of perfume: Je Reviens.

The bathroom has bright yellow everything.

Our basement is wide open and echoes. Mom has painted white hopscotch squares on the red cement floor. Dad has built shelves for books and puzzles and games like Steps 'n' Chutes. A hula hoop hangs from a steel bolt in the wall. My sisters and I play house with empty cardboard boxes. We have invisible children who misbehave. There is a real chalkboard and three wooden desks with inkwells for playing school. A toy box holds roller skates, tap-dancing shoes and crinolines for dress-up.

I am afraid of that crawl space under the stairs. What hides behind those golf clubs in checkered bags, the steamer trunk and brown suitcase filled with Christmas decorations? Blue flames flicker in the furnace that groans on and off. The hot water tank gurgles and hisses. Between the washer and dryer by the drain hose lives a white-haired, wrinkled, bug-eyed troll like in my book of Grimms' fairy tales. He could snatch my ankles if I don't scoot fast enough up the stairs. I yank the cord on the light bulb, return the dark to the basement—and run.

Up the stairs and out the back door is the backyard with flat square lawn for croquet or running through the sprinkler. There is a swing set and sandbox on the driveway by the back lane. A little sidewalk loops around to the front beside flowerbeds of columbines and peonies. Here the lawn slopes gently—perfect for continuous somersaults. Sometimes, at dusk, we play frozen tag or kick the can with the older kids on the block. My best friend and I hide behind the garbage cans, breathless, hearts pounding in our chests. They will never find us here.

"Time to come home!" My mother's voice echoes from a distant front porch.

It is nighttime in my bedroom.

I watch bright rectangles of light dart around the corners of my room. Headlight beams from passing cars.

I am afraid of the dark behind the closet. The heavy doors roll like thunder.

I hear the noisy breathing of my sister. She may be a good sleeper but she wets the bed.

I am afraid of being the last one to fall asleep.

A witch lives under my bed at night. If I look, she will scramble up the other side out of sight. She has striped stockings like the wicked witch that Dorothy's house landed on.

I am afraid of the big slide at the park two blocks away. It has BLUE IMP stamped on each rung that I climb. Some nights, I dream I am being chased by a giant and I fall from the top of the slide.

I am *not* afraid of the merry-go-round spinning faster and faster, the fine grey dust shooting up as we lay on our stomachs playing pickup sticks. I never get dizzy.

I am afraid of the deep end of the swimming pool.

I am afraid of big dogs. If they drool, they have rabies.

I am afraid of strangers with beards because they are kidnappers.

I am afraid of getting lost...

I hear sniffling and sobbing at the edge of my roll call of fears. Robin is fast asleep. It must be Kim, crying in her bedroom across the hallway.

I get out of bed to tell Mom, who is folding laundry while she watches *Perry Mason*. I recognize the brassy, sinister theme music of grown-up TV.

"Kim's crying." I know that Mom will go and comfort her.

But she doesn't. She snaps wrinkles from tea towels, folds them into smooth rectangles stacked on the arms of the chair.

I say it again, louder. "Kim is crying."

I see the wrinkles disappear from Mom's forehead. She is getting cross.

I didn't kill him, Mr. Mason. Believe me, I didn't.

"Go back to bed," she snaps. "Now."

I scurry down the hall, stung by her words. Why wasn't Mom helping Kim?

I'm just trying to determine the facts, ma'am. Just the facts.

Kim's drama unfolds without us.

She was miserable at school. Acceleration—that bold experiment for brainy kids—had been a disaster. Not only was she failing school, she had lost all her childhood friends.

My dad, noting this losing-friends trend, bought her Dale Carnegie's *How to Win Friends and Influence People*.

Twelve years old and midway through grade eight, Kim had made a decision. She would transfer to that Catholic boarding school for girls a few miles south of the city. She could come home on weekends to visit. There would be new friends and uniforms and choirs singing "Carol of the Bells." She would try those six ways to make people like you. *Smile. Be a good listener. Make the other person feel important* . . .

Maybe she will study more.

(Mom is so pleased. She says she would have given her eye teeth for a chance to go to boarding school with the nuns.)

On this night, just one week before she is supposed to leave, Kim stares into the dark of her bedroom. She can't fall asleep. Familiar tendrils of fear wrap around her throat. She takes a big breath, then another. Is she hyperventilating? Heartbeat pounds in her ears. Allegro. Presto. Stomach swirls—is she going to be sick? What if this happens at boarding school? Terrified, she confesses to Mom that she cannot leave home. Furious, Mom leaves her bedside and closes the door.

Left alone to cry in her blue room, Kim holds on tight to Butch the Dog and promises herself that, someday, she will be brave enough to leave.

Five years later, Kim left. My mother, father and I watched her figure become a pinpoint as she walked down the long corridor of the University of Lethbridge, shedding childhood and Kingsland as she walked.

"She looks so small," Mom said sadly. Earlier that morning, she lay down beside my sister as she slept. Was this a valediction or an offer of last-minute deliverance? Kim, suddenly awake and ramrod-straight beside her, knew there was no need for rescue. She could take care of herself.

We have the truth on our side, Mr. Mason.

{ THREE }

I
F OUR HOUSE was a castle, then our mother was
the queen.

If our mother was the queen, then we were royal children: sheltered and slightly spoiled. Presents from Santa
appeared magically Christmas mornings. Teddy bears,
dollhouses, new pajamas. There were summer holidays in
Jasper and Banff and Radium Hot Springs, where we could
eat in restaurants and stay at motels with swimming pools.
We had a cairn terrier named Haggis, spoiled as well. There
were Royal Conservatory piano lessons for Kim and me

and Speech Arts for Robin, who wore dresses of velvet and taffeta for her prize-winning recitations at the Kiwanis Music Festival.

Like a wicked stepsister, I envied everything about Robin. Her glossy dark hair bounced with ringlets, if my mother had her way, or braids, if Robin did. She could run fast and scale fences and throw a baseball like a boy. She could be teacher's pet without even trying. She held my mother's heart.

It was hard to stay jealous of Robin for any length of time, since she thought up the best games, like animal school or hospital with our twenty-six stuffed toys cast as pupils or patients. We played town & farm for hours on the brown indoor-outdoor carpet on the basement floor. Robin created her town around a toy gas station, Matchbox cars and a truck full of blue plastic dogs. She made miniature paper merchandise for the grocery and liquor stores and laid out the roadways with Tinkertoys. Out on the farm, I had a red barn full of plastic pigs, cows, sheep and chickens arranged in bucolic tableaux around fences and trees and way too tiny farm people. Occasionally, they would truck into town for supplies and Red Cap beer, our dad's favourite.

My best friend Karen lived two doors down. Every morning, I'd rush over, cutting across old Mr. Marshall's lawn. He tried a variety of devices to keep us from shortcutting: rope strung between trees, wire fences, even electric stakes that zapped dew worms.

Karen lived in a house cluttered with possibilities.

Drawings and finger paintings by all four children hung on yellow kitchen walls next to van Gogh's sunflowers. A ceramic duck cookie jar was filled with snickerdoodles. They had a built-in china cabinet and a clothes chute and a big stereo that stacked records and plunked them—one by one—onto the turntable below. They had the first automatic dishwasher on the block and after that, a new baby brother.

Karen's bedroom was lilac with poufy curtains and rumpled quilts. She shared it with her younger sister, so there were two of most things on the dresser. Two lacy lampshades with crystal bases. Two jewelry boxes with plastic ballerinas that twirled to music. Karen was a ballerina. She had long ash blond hair, hazel eyes and perfect teeth. I dreamed of being the piano accompanist for her performances.

I didn't like to share Karen with anyone, especially her little sister.

Their closet floor was a jumble of Barbies with naked limbs, doll clothes spilling out of a checkered pasteboard suitcase. Karen's Chatty Cathy had wild hair and a dangling pull cord. There were orange toy telephones that really worked for secret conversations down hallways, but the batteries were dead.

(The bedroom I shared with my sister was always tidy. Our twin beds had smooth matching bedspreads. Our closet floor held no surprises and smelled of Johnson paste wax. My Chatty Cathy sat primly in a little chair. Our Barbies lived in their vinyl cases, staring up beside their carefully packed wardrobes.)

Karen and I would spend entire days together, the angle of the sunshine through the windows changing morning to afternoon. Sometimes we were allowed to use the Mixmaster to make a Twinkle cake mix. We'd sing, "Someone left the cake out in the rain, I don't think that I can take it, 'cause it took so long to bake it, and I'll never have that recipe again."

Every now and then, Karen's mom would load all the kids into the station wagon and we'd be off for picnics in the country, the dust from gravel roads scudding behind us. We arrived in magical places with turquoise blue waterfalls and sun-warmed rock. Karen's mom knew all about wildflowers and birds and berries. We picked rose petals to make jam.

When Karen's dad came home from work downtown, he'd ask, "Where's the prettiest dollies on the block?" Then he'd scoop up his two daughters to tickle and kiss them. Catching sight of me, he'd chant the rhyme that always made me glow: "Midget Mary, quite contrary, how does your garbage grow?" Then he would kiss his wife, who always went to greet him at the door. They were so romantic.

One day, Karen's dad brought his girls home a present. Two pairs of high-heeled plastic shoes with tulle bows and peep-toes. They were translucent pink with flecks of gold. Glamorous shoes that dancers or movie stars might wear.

I wished my dad worked downtown.

My dad worked downstairs.

The western hub of Pyrotenax of Canada Limited was in our basement. In a room of pine-panelled walls, white acoustic ceiling tiles and a floor of red and black linoleum squares—one yellow square set whimsically at its centre—Dad set up his solo sales-rep operation.

The desk was a heavy plywood board set on two squat green metal filing cabinets. Three drawers for business accounts and one drawer for family matters and his so-called Wastepaper File, a collection of news clippings about the space race and airplane crashes mostly, along with stories of transgressions in the Catholic Church hierarchy and quirky how-to's. Dad liked to show visitors his article from a 1937 *Popular Mechanics* magazine on the "swinging gate method" of improving one's golf swing.

On shelves made of planks and yellow bricks, Dad set his collection of Alexander Hamilton's *Modern Business*, the encyclopedia of electrical wiring and a book called *When You Marry*. Back issues of *Road & Track* were stacked in a corner. Maps of Canada and the world were tacked to the walls beside framed certificates from International Correspondence Schools. Later, Dad would hang photographs of the import cars he'd owned, his beloved Rovers and Peugeots, alongside a photo of Haggis, the dog.

Since Dad was his own office help, he had all sorts of intriguing supplies: mechanical pencils, X-Acto knives, fountain pens and staplers that disappeared while we were playing school next door. "I've got an APB out for my stapler," he used to call out in good humour. There were stacks of brown and white envelopes with the bright red Pyrotenax letterhead and memo forms of pink and yellow paper with sooty carbons in between. A grey Remington manual typewriter sat on a portable table. This was a Christmas gift my father gave to my mother. Apparently, she gave it back to him in exchange for a brand new television.

In the far corner of Dad's downstairs office, set apart from the territorial responsibilities of Pyrotenax, was an alto saxophone on its metal claw stand. Back when Dad was ten, the barber in Whitewood got him started in the local boys' band. Our nights were filled with the sounds of Dad playing his saxophone downstairs. A swing counterpoint to our bedside prayers.

Our house was a castle and our mother was the queen. Our father worked in the basement spinning copper wire into gold.

If our house was a castle, then our Kingdom stretched east to Macleod Trail—dagger-straight and raw with commerce. Car dealerships. Restaurants. Motor Inns. To the west, Elbow Drive meandered, lined with tall poplars and stately homes with names like Windover. To the south was Heritage Drive and the YMCA for swimming lessons. To the north, Glenmore Trail bordered on the sweetest place on earth: Chinook Shopping Centre.

Every Saturday morning, our family would drive to Chinook and witness the passage of seasons indoors. In spring, there would be trips to Woodward's sporting goods department, smelling of bike tires and plastic skipping ropes in lime green, hot pink and orange. We tried on baseball gloves, pounding our fists into the pockets because we played softball for the Kingsland Tiny-Mites.

In summer, there would be the Stampede pancake breakfast and countless visits to the Chinook Public Library in the lower mall with its smells of barber shop, shoe repair and french fries from businesses nearby. The library was a sacred space—hushed except for the click of the microfiche camera or the distant thunder from the bowling alley. I remember thinking that the librarians wrote all the books. The dark-haired lady with the whispery voice was my favourite author: Lois Lenski.

Every fall, there would be back-to-school sales and brand new Laurentian pencil crayons that I would ferret away in my dresser drawer. Exotic colours like Hollywood Cerise, Arizona Topaz and Sarasota Orange in among my white cotton undershirts.

Every winter, we would wait impatiently for the gradual arrival of Christmas at Chinook Centre. In early December, giant candy canes were suspended from concrete pillars outside Woodward's. On the flat roof above Penley's Drugs a Night Before Christmas display was assembled, piece by piece, with agonizing slowness. First, the red-brick fireplace and chimney appeared. A week or so later, three cartoonish kids in nightgowns and nightcaps joined the scene. The next week, there would be stockings hanging in a row on the mantle. On Christmas Eve, our family would go for a car ride down Macleod Trail past Chinook Centre. Dad driving, Mom smiling, three girls bursting with excitement in the back seat. Santa Claus would finally be there, high atop the chimney. Plywood and paint, but magic just the same.

Inside Chinook Centre, there was a real Santa in his Toyland castle who gave you a colouring book and button if you were brave enough to sit on his lap. There were telephones to the North Pole where you could listen to Rudolph or Frosty the Snowman. Overhead, choirs of angels perched on clouds of pink and blue candy floss—much better than church.

Chinook Centre we could share as a family. For church, we splintered into factions. Mom was devoutly Catholic and Dad decidedly agnostic. They had agreed, however, that we three girls would be raised Catholic. Sunday mornings would find us driving south on Elbow Drive to St. Gerard's Church, our mother gripping the steering wheel of her white Chevrolet Epic, hell-bent for nine o'clock Mass.

St. Gerard's Church began where the city once ended. A farm with a big yellow barn was in the church's backyard. A new church was built in time for my First Communion. In 1967, this was a tribute to modern architecture and the modern church. There was a dark-skinned Jesus on the new cross that looked nothing like the fair, golden-haired Jesus in my *Good Manners in God's House: A First Book for Little Catholics*.

In the new church, the altar faced the congregation. The priests said the Mass in English instead of Latin. There was young, handsome Father Harrison and the old Monseigneur, who trembled when he gave out Communion wafers. Adults whispered it was because of all the changes. It was because of Vatican II.

During Mass, our mother recited the prayers with perfect diction and pace, just slightly ahead of the rest of the congregation. She sang in spite of her admitted lack of tone and glared our way if we didn't. In later years—once women were allowed into church proceedings apart from choirs and bake sales—she became head lector and manned (as she called it) the overhead projector.

At home, Mom was discreet with demonstrations of her faith. There was a Kitchen Prayer plaque by the stove that began "Oh Lord of all these pots and pans." She hung a holy calendar from Universal Church Supply in the hall closet with the floor polisher and dust mop.

Like most of her personal life, my mother kept her faith guarded and private. Stowed in her jewelry box were relics of a bygone Catholicism: a worn leather missal, a rosary, holy cards and a green felt scapular of the Blessed Virgin Mary on a string—a talisman for conversion. Each night, my mother knelt beside her bed, head in hands. It scared me to see her like this. Anguished. Alone. Like Jesus in Gethsemane.

As children, we had sunnier Catholic rituals. We had plastic crucifixes above our beds with rosaries looped around Jesus on the cross. We prayed nightly to guardian angels and for the poor souls in Purgatory. And we prayed for our father to convert.

(Dad never even set foot in St. Gerard's until my best friend's wedding years later. Sitting beside me, he leafed through the daily missal, remarking that the funeral Mass was first. "That's pretty bad PR," he chuckled.)

I liked being Catholic, even though we didn't have a stern father to complete our family pew or lead us in meal-time grace. I liked the dignified hymns, the murmur of rote prayer, the punctuation of sit, stand, kneel. I liked the accessories: white gloves, little purses and straw hats with grosgrain ribbons dangling down the back. I liked to

watch the women's shoes inch past our pew in the Communion line-up, my head bowed in reverence over my *Good
Manners* storybook:

*You are no longer just a plain child. Every girl is a princess in
the Church of God.*

We lorded our Catholic superiority over the Protes-
tant kids in our neighbourhood ("You're going to Hell!")
and bragged about our holy holidays when they had to go
to school.

But those dreaded trips to Confession kept us relatively
contrite.

The lights above the confessional cubicles glow red as
each sinner kneels inside. I wait in line rehearsing my lines
—stomach swirling, head swimming—afraid I'll forget.

"Forgive me, Father, for I have sinned. It has been four
weeks since my last Confession. These are my sins: Fighting
with sisters. Saying 'Hell.' Stealing a quarter for candy. May
God the Father forgive me and make me true to His Spirit."

That huge relief afterward could only mean redemption.
The black marks on my soul have disappeared, like an Etch-
a-Sketch turned upside down and shaken.

(Not until my sisters and I began university did Dad
feel the time had come to rattle our Catholic chains. Across
the dining room table set for Christmas or Easter dinners,
he would challenge us to defend our religion with his favourite gambits: "How do you explain the dinosaurs?" or "How
can the Pope be infallible?" We had our own doubts by
then, anyway.)

The outside world never ventured far inside our ten
blocks of Kingsland. Like royalty, we were sheltered from

life's complications. A fleet of friendly breadmen, milkmen and mailmen patrolled the streets. Paperboys tossed news of the outside in. Parents poured themselves a drink and retreated behind newsprint walls. Children were sent out to play.

As long as we stayed in the Kingdom, we would always be safe.

{ FOUR }

WHILE THE YOUTH of the world was meeting at Haight-Ashbury for the Summer of Love, I was an eight-year-old, pedalling my bike toward home through the Calgary dusk wondering what, exactly, a hippie was.

The topic of hippies had come up at our supper table earlier that evening. It was the one meal when we were all together. Suppertime was Discussion Time and my father often took this opportunity to educate us in his own fashion—a kind of mealtime Socrates—away from my mother's overarching routines of homework and piano practice.

Dad's lessons were brief and didactic, with regular features—not unlike *Reader's Digest* magazine. "Increase Your Word Power" was our vocabulary drill. "What does *ubiquitous* mean?" Dad would ask in his loud voice. There was "Humour in Uniform" where Dad would share the jokes he'd heard while on his sales calls that day. "What did the rary in the wheelbarrow say when it looked over the cliff? That's a long way to tip-a-rary!" (We needed that one explained.)

Even as we grew older and the boy down the lane had got a girl pregnant, the "Drama in Real Life" cautionary lecture emerged at the supper table. "Just look what can happen after ten minutes of pleasure!" Dad exhorted. My mother rattled the dishes loudly in the sink. *She* would handle the facts of life, thank you very much.

(And she had. Books wrapped in thick plastic envelopes appeared on our beds one day. *What Teenagers Want to Know* was for Kim. Robin read *A Doctor Talks to Nine- to Twelve-Year-Olds* after shoving me out of our room and slamming the door. "You're too young!" Mom and I read *The Story of Life* together. She sat rigid-backed on my bed as we looked at drawings of flowers and bees.)

But about these hippies. My parents seemed concerned, no, alarmed by the rumours of this new edginess in Banff. I turned the word over in my head—hippies, hippos, zoo—and was totally confused about what had overrun the mountain tourist spot. All I'd ever seen Banff overrun with was old people leaning against the edges of the smelly Sulphur Mountain Hot Springs pool.

At home and school, we celebrated the progress of the 1960s. Man on the moon. Colour television. Shatterproof shampoo bottles. Flower Power meant love beads, tie-dye shirts and bell-bottoms. The Vietnam War and the demonstrations against it were distant, violent events that could never happen in Canada.

Could they?

By 1970, I was beginning to worry about the world.

It came to me gradually through a quirky gestalt of these suppertime discussions, Simon and Garfunkel songs and a *Book of Knowledge* I'd won in a colouring contest. Glossy photographs showed the year in review. Dead fish lying in suds-filled water. Phosphates. Smokestacks spewing grime into the atmosphere. Smog. Landfills teaming with garbage and gulls. Pollution.

I brought up my concerns at the supper table and felt a flicker of approval from Dad. Here I was speaking with intelligence and logic. By discussing Important Issues, my father believed we would grow into good judges of character and responsible citizens. We decided, as a family, to buy phosphate-free laundry detergent.

I went public with my concerns, entering an essay contest about what I would change in my hometown. I imagined myself in the Husky Tower "looking fondly on the city below" to warn the people of Calgary about what progress was doing to the environment. I won another *Book of Knowledge* and got my picture in the paper. The essay made its way back to *The Calgary Herald*, where the columnist wrote this question above his daily brickbats and bouquets: "Didn't eleven-year-old girls used to worry about hopscotch?"

Even Kingsland was changing. My best friend's older brother grew his hair long, argued with his mother and made her cry. He played guitar and smoked, disappearing into his basement bedroom with its wall-to-wall photos cut from *Time* and *Life* magazines. I heard rumours about other teenagers in the neighbourhood. Runaways. Drug addicts.

Hippies.

I knew that my own sister, Robin, had started smoking. Part of the junior high code for popularity. She quit Speech Arts after numerous dramatic rages at Mom, who surrendered, silent and bitter. I snooped in Robin's diary and eavesdropped on her phone calls trying to figure out this sullen, moody stranger. At home, she insulted me. At school, she ignored me. I wanted the old Robin back.

My best friend Karen stopped being my best friend in a spate of nasty phone calls and "We hate you's" yelled down the lane. A girl in Karen's ballet class led the insurrection. We'd been competing for best friend status since grade two. I still didn't like to share Karen with anyone. "You lead people around by the nose," Karen announced and strode up the back lane, ever the prima ballerina, without me.

Our walks to school along streets made safe with company and conversation ended. On my own, I was afraid of the big junior high kids in their lumberjack flannel shirts who smoked in the back alley behind the school and wouldn't let you pass unless you gave them candy from Pete's Confectionary.

"Surrender your Dubble Bubble. Give up your Lik-M-Aid."

Late one afternoon, I went back to school to get a book I'd forgotten, walking alone across the deserted tarmac where we played Chinese skipping each recess. Brad—the worst kid in our grade six class—was hanging around by the boot room doors. He'd been strapped. He'd been suspended. He'd been flunked. It had only made him meaner.

He sauntered up to me, his thin wiry body hunched in a jean jacket. Hands shoved into pockets.

"School's over," he sneered, his dark eyes squinting in a hawkish face. I felt my stomach twist with fear—but knew better than to show it.

"I forgot my homework," I giggled.

"Such a goody-goody," he said in baby talk, moving in to block my way.

He brought his face in close to mine. There was a dark mole on his cheek. Thin lips stretched into a grin.

He jammed his fingers against the crotch of my jeans.

What was he doing?

He tickled me. Down *there*.

Flustered, frightened, I giggled again.

"Did you like that?" he laughed and pushed me toward the door, my face hot with shame, relieved he hadn't punched me.

I never told a soul.

Every morning after I woke to the dread of that solitary walk. Stomach in knots, I'd plead to stay home from school.

"Take half this Donnatal tablet," said my mother, offering me her prescription blend for tummy troubles.

"Seems like she has a migraine stomach," remarked Dr. Mahoney as he wheeled his stool away from me, shivering in my undershirt, and turned to my mother, sitting solicitously across from the examination table. "Give her milk of magnesia every morning and night."

Thick white awful peppermint chalk. There had to be a better way.

I made a new friend to walk to school with instead. An auxiliary friendship that would last until Karen returned.

Until order was restored in the Kingdom.

⌂ ⌂ ⌂

SUDDENLY, I DIDN'T WANT to grow up.

No. I *did* want to grow up. I had dreams for a handsome blond husband and adorable blond children in a two-storey house like Samantha's on *Bewitched*. I had the adult part all mapped out. What I didn't want was the in-between time: being a teenager. Acne. Arguments with parents. All that peer pressure to smoke, take drugs and neck with boys.

I needed a plan.

I went for a walk up the back lane on a cold, clear night. The moon reflected off the snow, making everything bright. I talked to myself out loud in the stillness and picked up a small rock to anchor my intentions. Later, I would spray-paint it silver and print the letters SDC-TLF on it with black magic marker. This was my private code for *No Sex* (before marriage, of course) *No Drugs* and *No Cigarettes*. I added *True Love Forever* because that's what adulthood would bring when all this "adolescence" was done. I put my rock in a Gold Nuggets chewing-gum pouch and stuffed it with yellow Easter grass. This rock would stem the rushing, changing waters around me.

I would not be moved.

My sisters were beyond redemption.

When Kim returned from university for semester breaks and holidays, she carried a green army-surplus knapsack, a guitar and a string of temperamental boyfriends with long hair who wrote poetry or music. She also brought a book called *Our Bodies, Ourselves: A Book by and for Women* that I pored over in horror-filled fascination. Body parts I'd never seen and experiences I'd never heard of were presented in photographs and detailed text. There was more to the facts of life than our plastic-wrapped trilogy had let on!

When I saw a package of birth-control pills in Kim's purse, I decided that leaving home was morally dangerous. When she moved in with her professor and stopped visiting altogether, I decided that leaving home was betrayal.

Meanwhile, my sister Robin had acquired a long-haired boyfriend of her own. She began cutting high school classes and hanging out anywhere but home. I found a plastic film canister of marijuana in one of her jackets I'd borrowed without asking. I was stunned and scared for her but never told anyone. Late one weekend, the police brought her home in their cruiser. I woke up the next morning to a house wrapped tight with silence. Robin, outwardly defiant, inwardly mortified, set her sights on the day when she could leave home for good.

It is my mother who cries at night now. Heaving sobs, rasping sounds from machinery that has rusted shut. I am sixteen and have never heard my mother cry like this. I tap on her bedroom door and speak into darkness. "Mom, what's the matter?" No answer. More of that horrible rasp. "Mom, what's wrong?"

It is wrenching—this sudden role reversal. My mother is supposed to be the strong one. I'm the one who falls apart after dark. My mother is the one who listens to the stories of runaways and junkies who are other people's children and says "Oh dear" and "Poor thing" in all the right places.

Her words come between sobs. "Everything I do fails."

The silence is thick and black and damp. I rush words into place. List the good things: health, home, relatively okay kids. (This struck me as a thin variation on my mother's response to my own jags of teenage sadness: "Be thankful. You could be in a wheelchair.")

I make her some tea. I will not disappoint my mother. She has not failed.

△ △ △

NEARLY TEN YEARS LATER, on this Sunday evening in August, my sister Kim has phoned to say, "I know why you're not sleeping."

She tells me about the night I'd heard her crying in her room. Mom folding laundry. *Perry Mason* on TV. I never knew my sister's side of the story.

"I cried myself to sleep that night. But I promised myself that someday I would be brave enough to leave."

Distanced by time and place and choice, my sister gives me absolution.

"It's all right to leave Mom."

That night I fall gently, effortlessly asleep. Next night, same thing. And the night after that.

The insomnia has released me.

It is all right to leave.

△ △ △

I REMEMBER THE FIRST TIME on my bike without the training wheels.

Lifting my leg over the crossbar, I straddled the seat. One foot up. One foot down. Determined, anxious, waiting for my sister's start-up push on my back. Pedal. Wobble. Fall. Try again. And again.

Then one day it happened, that magic sensation of balance and glide, a smile spreading like sun across my face. I wanted to look back and shout "I'm riding by myself!" but I stared at the road ahead, tongue out in concentration, handlebar streamers flapping an applause.

I never told my mother about that either.

PART 2

{ FIVE }

THE NURSE GIVES ME the key to the washroom, along with an empty Styrofoam cup. The key jangles and clanks on its large metal ring as I walk down the hall and up the stairs. I step inside the cubicle, slide the latch across, sit down and begin to cry.

Later, back in the waiting room, the nurse crosses two fingers into a plus sign, a discreet little signal that makes the room spin.

Our family doctor's office was downtown in a brown brick building with heavy revolving doors. Dr. Mahoney had managed my health from birth through adulthood. His gravelly, sonorous voice could penetrate examining room walls into the waiting room where polite patients and the nurse in her crisp white cap pretended not to hear. No health issue ever felt private with Dr. Mahoney and he always seemed to give the same advice: "Soak it in Epsom salts." Ankle. Head. Heart.

Thankfully, a younger, more soft-spoken doctor had recently joined the practice.

He meets with me in his office to discuss my situation. Adult to adult. Matter-of-fact. Unaware of all my ailments in that overstuffed file folder on his desk. He suggests that I might feel more comfortable seeing a woman doctor. His wife is taking new maternity patients.

I hadn't planned on getting pregnant. I was still working on the getting serious phase when everything went tilt.

I'd always been careful with precautions although that night on the Thanksgiving weekend, I don't remember being concerned. We were in the midst of long-distance relationship highs and lows and had thrown caution to the wind.

We had met in university and had reconnected through a number of chance meetings I saw as serendipitous. I had just ended a long relationship. He was similarly single. So we went to a Billy Joel concert together. The next day, we played squash and went swimming. We planned to ski the next weekend. That was how our courtship began.

Every Friday night, we would pick up where we'd left off the weekend before. I worked hard at being fun and athletic all the time, grafting a whole new dimension onto my personality that left me—between whirlwind weekends—physically exhausted and intensely insecure.

This must be love.

Every Friday night, I'd keep us both awake discussing where the relationship was headed. By Saturday, I'd feel guilty about the hassle I'd caused by bringing up the word "commitment" and resolve to be more fun. Less needy.

Sex helped.

By Sunday, we'd have reconnected. He would resume his life a hundred miles away and I'd resume mine, reluctantly, in Calgary.

He was in no rush to commit. In his other life, he worked, skied, sailed and shared an apartment with three other teachers—all of whom were female, attractive and much better athletes than me.

(I would like to blame my jealous flaw on my sister, Robin, although I know it really isn't her fault for having received the superior physical package. It came with its own set of risks that I didn't know about then. All I know is that I'd grown up with the surprised reaction of friends, teachers, co-workers—even my own boyfriends—when they discovered Robin and I were sisters: "But you don't look at all alike!"

I called this the "Barbie and Midge syndrome."

Barbie was created by the Mattel Toy Company in 1959. Her best friend, Midge, was created in 1963. Despite their age difference, they had a lot in common: identical bodies with hard plastic breasts, tiny waists and those impossibly long legs ending in permanently pointed toes. You could inter-change their heads with a satisfying little pop and they fit each other's outfits perfectly: cocktail frocks, pedal-pushers, natty two-piece suits.

But Midge wasn't Barbie—despite these similarities. Midge had stiff orange-red hair in a permanent flip and a fringe of bangs. She had saucer-round blue eyes and freck-les. Barbie had curly poodle bangs and long blond hair you could swirl into a bun or ponytail. She had indigo eyes lined with eyeshadow that arched upward. Catlike bedroom eyes.

Barbie was glamorous. Midge was not.

Even the illustrations on their black vinyl carrying cases told this story. Barbie, dressed in a strapless evening gown, sings in front of a microphone. Midge stands demurely in a modest two-piece swimsuit of lime green and orange. In another picture, Barbie looks chic in après-ski-wear. Midge looks prissy in a skating skirt. No wonder this boring best friend never stood a chance with Ken.

As long as there was a Barbie in sight, I would always be a Midge.)

◊ ◊ ◊

ONTO THIS UNSETTLED romantic relationship front moved gale force winds. My period, usually punctual, was late.

Could I be pregnant?

Probably not—but we might as well make sure.

We bought a home pregnancy test at a super-drug-mart where we could be a carefree, anonymous couple. Back in my apartment, he read the instructions with mock seriousness. I giggled from the bathroom, tinkling on the plastic stick.

He timed the results as we talked about cycling in Europe the next summer or teaching overseas someday. Maybe I could write for magazines about our travelling adventures.

Blue.

Unmistakably.

Blue.

Irrevocably.

He confirmed it.

I denied it.

He said this was kind of neat.

I said this wasn't supposed to happen yet. We were still working on being a couple when suddenly, accidentally, we were going to be three.

Dazed, we went through the motions of the rest of our Sunday afternoon. Shopped at the mall for Halloween costumes to wear to school the next day. I dressed up as nothing-in-particular and joined the costume parade winding through school hallways. Witches and Snow Whites and human crayons. I would be waking up from this dream any minute.

◊ ◊ ◊

I LIE ON the examining table, knees bent, heels in cold stirrups, white sheet pulled up to my chin. I am pissed off at my body—out on this spur line without my permission.

My new woman doctor offers a different perspective. "We don't really have control over our bodies," she said, peeling off her latex gloves. "Some people learn that lesson by getting MS or cancer. You get to have a baby."

I bury the wonder with worries: "But I'm not married. I teach in a Catholic school. What will people think?"

"This is none of their business."

Evidently, she's never read *Good Manners in God's House.*

New doctor. New life. New choices.

I was twenty-nine years old. How could I *not* have control over my body? I'd been working on control since I was twelve.

Since my first menstrual period, in fact, which began during my piano lesson. I stared—stunned and a little queasy—at my bloodstained terry cloth shorts. I broke the news to Mom in the privacy of the yellow bathroom. She hugged me and shared her girlhood memory of fainting from cramps on the railway tracks.

A sanitary belt and box of Kotex napkins magically appeared on my bed—a gift from the feminine hygiene fairy. I asked my sister Robin how to rig it all up, eager to let her know that I was now part of the sorority. Disgusted, she locked the bulky pad into the belt clips and snapped it, slingshot-style, across the bed.

"There!"

Puberty flooded in with all the murky, sloggy feelings promised in the *Girl to WOMAN* film we watched in health class, the projector chattering in the dark, the story unfolding in the dull commentary and corny acting of the decade before. The boys were in another room watching *Boy to MAN*.

This was unfortunate. When it came to boys and men, I knew nothing more than the layered Cellophane anatomy pages in the *Encyclopedia Britannica* where I pressed my autumn leaves, although I *had* seen the private parts of the boy down the lane when I was five. His mother heard us snickering in the closet. I was sent home to kneel in front of my plastic crucifix and tell Jesus I was sorry.

My own father was a mystery, physically speaking. At my mother's insistence, he built a bathroom downstairs, where he performed what he called his daily ablutions, away from our curious female stares.

It seemed my whole body had begun to betray me. For someone who'd learned all the words to "I Enjoy Being a Girl" at age seven—and sang them with conviction—I had been hoping for better things.

My skin broke out everywhere. I frightened myself with the prospect of a face, scarred and pitted, like my science teacher, who was single and seemed lonely. I pleaded with Mom to take me to a dermatologist, who drew diagrams of hair follicles and sprayed my face with ice-cold nitrogen.

I hated my short, mousy brown hair more than ever after a substitute teacher mistook me for a boy. I wanted long straight hair parted down the middle like Julie on *The Mod Squad*. In my romantic future daydreams, I always had long blond hair and clear skin.

Getting me "good hair" had been an ongoing project for my mother—who cursed her own thin wisps and said that mine were just the same. As a child, she had consumed countless bread crusts in an effort to make her hair Shirley Temple curly. She started me early on a regimen of pixie cuts to make my hair thicker. I would sit on the high chair in our kitchen and feel the big silver sewing shears munch unsteadily across my Scotch-taped bangs. For special occasions, Mom would curl my hair with crisscrossed bobby pins—consolation kiss curls for those of us with hair too short for pink sponge rollers.

Our good-hair goal was helped along by Toni home permanents. Mom would twist hanks of my hair into blue, pink and white plastic rods, arranging them symmetrically—just like the instructions showed—across my aching scalp. After twenty minutes of eye-watering, ammonia-soaked anticipation, I would bend over the edge of the bathtub to be neutralized and rinsed.

The result?

Disastrous. Nothing like the photo on the box.

"Did you stick your finger in an electric socket?" my father would joke at the supper table.

I'd feel hot, angry tears gather in my throat. "I hate this!" I'd tug at the frizzy curls. "I hate this!"

"Go to your room."

There was no place for tears or tantrums at the supper table. Hysteria, Dad would remind us, comes from the Greek word for womb. At times, women have uncontrollable emotions.

△ △ △

NOVEMBER, COLD AND GREY, descended. At the end of each day of teaching, I would return, bone-tired, emotionally spent, to my attic apartment in an old house in South Calgary. This had been the perfect character apartment when I'd moved in a few months earlier. Now, the smell of damp wood and musty gas heaters made the morning sickness rise in waves. Wind whined through holes in the window sashes. Tree branches clawed at the panes. Pipes shuddered and froze. Bathwater sat for days in the old-fashioned claw-footed tub.

I had banished myself to the cold, lonely house at the top of the hill.

◊ ◊ ◊

MY BOYFRIEND AND I discussed our options over brunch at a restaurant where, two years earlier, we had gone after our first night of exploratory sex. I felt clandestine and naughty then. Now I just felt hungry. And angry. Shoved into a set of decisions that had little to do with romance.

Somewhere in our conversation, he said, "Maybe we don't have to get married right away." Words that felt like freedom. We had a choice. We would have the baby—not a skiff of indecision there—then decide. Marriage, admittedly over-the-top in my imagination, was still about choosing each other.

I had taken my time with the selection process. Friends had been engaged, married—even divorced—in the time I was taking to find "the One."

My first love was my junior high gym teacher, who had a nice smile and biceps that bulged out of his T-shirt sleeves when he demonstrated chin-ups on the parallel bars. When he complimented me on my campaign speech for student council, I was smitten. I invented all sorts of reasons to hang around the gym: scorekeeping, timekeeping, tidying the equipment room. I knew the scent of his aftershave. I imagined our life together, growing myself up with soap-opera speed. I tried out for every team and joined the school gymnastics club. When I accidentally fell off the rings and· broke my arm, he visited me in the hospital, which seemed romantic and promising at the time. He asked me if I was keeping my food down.

In high school, I continued to fall for nice guys with smiles and biceps who actually noticed *me*—smart, sarcastic but deep. Not drop-dead gorgeous, mind you, but loads of personality.

This faith in the power of "perky" came from years of watching the *Miss Canada* pageant on TV with my mother, who reassured me that the most prestigious honour went to Miss Congeniality, who always seemed to come from the Maritimes. But by the time host Jim Perry began to sing *We've found her at last, the fairest girl in Canada,* Miss Congeniality was long forgotten, just another smiling, wretched face in the crowd around a beautiful, teary, tiara'd Miss Canada.

The arrival of the first steady boyfriend both surprised and unnerved my mother, who peered out her bedroom curtains if I lingered too long with goodnights in his car.

She ambushed me as I tiptoed through the dark hallway, quoting Ann Landers on *going too far*.

She didn't need to worry. I had my silver rock to ground me.

(I would abandon my no-sex-before-marriage edict a few years later when some girlfriends admitted they had been going too far for quite some time. We were sitting in a Jack in the Box restaurant in Honolulu during a university trip called "Bust Loose." Their disclosures—and the fact that they were good Catholic girls—freed me from my earlier choices, set, as they were, in spray-painted stone.)

It was time to tell to my mother.

Expecting news of an official engagement, she poured herself a Scotch and sat in anticipation at the kitchen table. She would have married this man herself, so great was their simpatico.

"I'm pregnant."

"Oh my God!" she gasped, covering her mouth with her hands.

The prodigal daughter, trying to make her way in the adult world, had failed and come home to mother.

"It wasn't supposed to happen this way." I was crying now. "I don't know what to do next."

Mom, her composure regained as mine dissolved, assured me that I didn't have to quit my job or leave town or take any of the other dire actions I'd been imagining. She would help and support us—whatever we decided.

Later she kissed my forehead, saying, "I know you wanted this to be different."

◌ ◌ ◌

MY PARENTS HAD MET in the Officers' Mess in North Bay, where my mother was the new teacher at the air force base school. Dad overhead her wisecracking with the cook. She wore a muskrat fur coat and deep V-neck sweater, her dark hair set in tight curls. She had a stage voice, comic face, antic gestures. "Now there's a meretricious thespian," my dad remarked to his bemused tablemates. A few weeks later, my mother asked him to the Valentine's Dance. Family legend has it that she did it on a dare.

Their courtship consisted of social events on the base and car rides in Dad's green 1950 Ford Meteor. This was the closest they would get to love written in the stars; my parents didn't have a lot in common. Mom was sociable and outgoing. She made excellent small talk and was an attentive listener. Dad preferred discussion and debate on current events and politics. Mom loved live theatre; Dad loved his music. At parties, Mom would jitterbug while Dad played his saxophone.

Their biggest stumbling block would be religion. Mixed marriages were discouraged by the Catholic Church but Mom was so desperate to have children that she put the rules aside. Temporarily.

They were married one year later in the manse of the United Church in Pemberton, Ontario. No guests. No reception. No fanfare. Their wedding was an offstage beginning to a marriage that would always be more pragmatic than romantic, more ready-to-wear than tailor-made. Our mother had been shopping for a solid, reliable guy. Our father was a forty-four regular off-the-rack.

I'd wanted my marriage to be different.

◇ ◇ ◇

I WAITED A LONG TIME to break the news to Dad. I knew that he approved of the man ("He knows how to handle you"), but I was afraid of his usual criticism: that I was flighty and failed to think ahead. ("Just look what can happen after ten minutes of pleasure!")

I have asked to speak with Dad alone. We sit at the kitchen table. He stirs sugar into his instant coffee, puzzled by this request from the youngest of his "bewildering offspring"—as he used to call us.

"I'm pregnant."

I wish that just once I could say those words without feeling stupid. Marvel at the miracle. Celebrate with hugs and kisses.

But Dad has never been one for displays of affection. He would rather change the oil in my car than give me a hug. He's never cuddled or coddled us. He rarely kissed us goodnight. I've never been his princess, dolly, sweetie or honey. He has always called me Midge—a name I share with an extremely small, potentially pesky, gnat-like insect.

Dad smiles a little.

"The same thing happened to my sister, Agnes."

The prim, thin aunt who sent us Avon talcum powder and a new two-dollar bill every birthday?

Dad nods.

"This happened back in the Hungry Thirties."

When we were little, Dad used to tell us bedtime stories about his boyhood in the southern Saskatchewan town of Whitewood. Summers at the cottage at Round Lake, his first ride in Uncle Hector's 1928 Ford Model A or the time he threw a tantrum in the toy department of Eaton's in Regina.

"I spotted a red Super Boy-Car and jumped in it. I told my mother, 'I won't get out until you buy it for me!' Which she did, eventually."

When Dad told stories, the sky of my imagination was always blue and the sun shone brightly on a scene not unlike the town & farm game we used to play.

By contrast, Mom's stories were dark, sad fragments. The Christmas with only a pair of mittens for a present. The day her new bicycle got repossessed. In her stories, the sky is always grey, trees stark.

"So my sister, Agnes, and Jimmy were courting," Dad continues in his orator's voice. "Agnes got pregnant but Jimmy was not allowed to marry until his employer, the Imperial Bank of Commerce, said he could."

Good jobs like this were hard to come by, Dad points out, parenthetically. He remembers seeing all the men out of work, down on their luck, riding the boxcars through town.

"So Agnes and Jimmy went down to the States one weekend and secretly got married. Agnes was sent to stay with relatives in Toronto until she had the baby. Then she returned to Whitewood to teach while the Toronto family raised her daughter."

"That must have been awful."

"Agnes went back to Toronto each summer to visit. When Jimmy enlisted in the army a few years later the family was reunited. By then, they had two daughters and a third on the way. These situations tend to have a good outcome," Dad concludes.

I knew my employers would be less draconian but I still worried over what they would expect me to do. I worked for the last institution on earth, it seemed, where pregnant and unmarried were anathema—except for the Virgin Mary. Would I be like my sixth grade teacher who mysteriously disappeared over the Christmas holidays?

"Sometimes," Dad says, "you have to live with some suspense."

◊ ◊ ◊

I TOLD MY PRINCIPAL. "I thought you'd have known better," he said.

I told the personnel director of the school board. "We should be bringing out the champagne and celebrating. You've decided to have this baby."

For an instant, I let myself feel proud.

"But things might be easier if you were married," he added.

A hasty marriage would be one way around my private minefield of (largely imagined) public scorn.

◊ ◊ ◊

MY OWN MOTHER had been born out of wedlock, the child of a stenographer named Jane Gordon and an unnamed man "high up" in politics. She was adopted as an infant by a married couple who had no children. For ten years, Patricia was their only child, doted on and adored. Then their son was born and, a year later, a daughter. The father abandoned the family soon after.

My mother believed these were her real parents until she discovered, at seventeen, some unfinished adoption papers stowed in a steamer trunk. Shocked and confused, she asked her mother, who, flustered and angry, yelled at her for snooping through things that were none of her business.

I didn't know this story until I was twenty. It knocked my world a little sideways as I scrolled through the dramatis personae of aunts, uncles and cousins who weren't. I'd liked being related to my grandmother Nan, with her blue Icelandic eyes and feisty, independent spirit, who had raised three children on her own.

That kind of courage was not in my blood after all.

△ △ △

I HAVE ALWAYS *been afraid.*

I am afraid of walking to school by myself. I wait for my best friend Karen as the time to leave for school stretches past, a sick feeling rising in my stomach at the thought of being late, or worse, walking the ten blocks alone.

I am not afraid of school.

I am in grade one. My fingernails are clean. I have brought a peach chiffon handkerchief from my mother's dresser drawer to lay my hands on for fingernail inspection. I print carefully and read stories with expression. We draw pictures of what we want to be when we grow up and I choose a nun. I work for days on the rosary my picture-nun wears around her neck. She has a bright yellow halo with rays like the sun.

When I am a grown-up, I will be brave.

△ △ △

I AM NOW a grown-up. Nothing like a nun. Afraid to do this on my own.

My boyfriend and I decide to get engaged and go to a French restaurant to celebrate. My little black dress—hallmark of a sexier former self—is tight over my stomach. As I expand, my life seems to shrink.

We shop at Christmas-crowded malls for an engagement ring. We sit in upholstered chairs in front of Windex'd display cases, where we are apprised of the four C's of diamond quality by smiling, ingratiating sales clerks.

This is not how I'd pictured it at all.

I once kept a collection of De Beers diamond advertisements torn from back issues of *Reader's Digest* magazines. They were photo stories with variations on the theme of "A diamond lasts forever." I would look through the ads whenever I felt a little shaky in my world. Surely things would be better when I grew up and found true love. My favourite ad showed a photo sequence of a young woman and her boy-friend, soon-to-be fiancé.

Frame one: *(establishing shot)* Handsome Blond Man with even teeth and Pretty Woman with long blond hair sitting on couch in nice apartment. Mad faces. Seem to be arguing.

Frame two: *(close-up shot)* Couple yelling at each other.

Frame three: *(long shot)* Woman walks out of apartment onto balcony.

Frame four: *(medium shot)* Man sitting alone on couch. Tie loosened. Hair tousled. Looks thoughtful. Remorseful.

Frame five: *(close-up)* Woman sniffling into lace hankie. Face attractively tear-streaked. Blue eyes sad.

Frame six: *(medium shot)* Man walking out through glass patio doors to girl on balcony.

Frame seven: *(close-up)* Man pulls strand of girl's long hair affectionately. Girl smiles through tears.

Frame eight: *(extreme close-up)* Man gives girl tiny velvet box.

Frame nine: *(extreme close-up that fills the rest of the page)* Big hug. Woman smiles through fresh tears. Eyes closed.

(Caption) "A diamond lasts forever."

The real-life circumstances for officially receiving my diamond ring were romantic enough. On Christmas morning, we went for a walk along the frozen river. Hoarfrost glistened on willows against a clear blue sky. The handsome blond man proposed. He was trying hard to do things right.

He got down on one knee. I laughed and cried, an undercurrent of sadness welling up. The ring was perfect.

Back at the house, we show his parents. They are thrilled.

We tell them we are pregnant. They make tea.

"Everything seems fine after a good cup of tea."

◠ ◠ ◠

JUST ABOUT EVERYONE—PARENTS, friends, colleagues—agreed things would be smoother if we got married sooner rather than later.

The wedding is set for a Friday evening in February. Six weeks away. This calls for a wedding of shortcuts.

Luckily, I have found a guidebook: *Bride's Shortcuts and Strategies for a Beautiful Wedding.*

Supermodel Kim Alexis dressed up as a radiant bride smiles at me from the front cover. I doubt she is pregnant. The book promises step-by-step instructions that will help me have the most beautiful wedding ever. I opt for the Thirty-Day Plan.

THE CHURCH

Fortunately, my fiancé's uncle is a Catholic priest who can expedite church rules about banns and marriage preparation courses. He's seen a range of human difficulties in his time. An o'erhasty marriage is no big deal. Since his new church is under construction, we will be married in an ATCO portable trailer, temporary home of the Church of the Holy Redeemer.

THE RECEPTION

A champagne reception is planned in the penthouse of a downtown hotel. Perfect for an intimate, elegant gathering that will suit the subdued nature of the celebration. No dinner. No dance. No silliness with garters and bouquets.

THE ATTENDANTS

My best friend Karen will be matron of honour. She has been married and divorced, and is in a new relationship. They have a baby daughter. I envy her world, her freedom to choose without judgment.

THE INVITATIONS

Karen's younger sister, an artist, designs our wedding invitation. Two cartoon penguins in wedding attire meet at a crossroads on Highway 2.

THE DRESS

My wedding dress and jacket of ivory wool and satin will be made by a designer friend who is unfazed by my constantly changing figure. "You've popped," she announces at my second-last fitting and sends me on a quest for a longline girdle at Woodward's.

I remember when my mother took me to the Woodward's foundations department to be fitted for a training bra. Together, we walked through the baby department and into the underworld of underwear, located discreetly between the beauty salon and the high racks of housecoats. I muttered a quick "Please God, don't let any boys I know see me."

I don't think men were even allowed in the foundations department at Woodward's. The ladies—capable, no-non-sense matrons—patrolled the department in their clinical white coats with tape measures draped around their necks. Lapel pins identified them as brassiere professionals. After all, Playtex had just revolutionized the world with cross-your-heart technology. We relied on these women to guide and support us—or at least our mothers did.

The brassiere professional focused on my emerging mounds, lassoed my bustline with her tape measure and sent me to undress in the fitting room. Four or five training bras were expertly shucked from their boxes and scooted through the crack in the door. Along with my mother.

She would be there to sanction nearly every rite of passage on my tentative journey toward womanhood. With one exception. And now look at the bind I was in.

THE PHOTOGRAPHER

The wedding portraits will be taken at a studio with various sets and props to choose from, like a faux marble fireplace on a Persian carpet. Perhaps a pergola or Roman ruin. Although this wedding has a shotgun feel to it, guns are not among the props.

THE REGISTRY

Gift decisions come next. The entire process strikes me as more than a little mercenary but my mother assures me that registering will take the guesswork out of giving. Late one January afternoon, I drop into Paris Jewelers, once a purple clapboard house where I got my ears pierced, now a brick monolith for china and crystal.

A saleslady scurries over.

"When is your wedding?" she inquires.

"In a month."

She is momentarily stunned. "That leaves very little time for registering properly."

"Yes," I agree. Should I mention that my prenatal class keeps getting in the way?

She points to the displays surrounding us, named for the discerning couples who have created personal statements through flatware, stemware and china. Beneath their names are the wedding dates—all a respectable distance in the future.

One such couple wanders through the store. He wears a navy melton cloth coat over his suit and tie. He has carefully styled hair and considers each plate through his wire-rimmed glasses. He discusses permutations of dishes with his well-heeled fiancée. This couple would never have a baby without similar forethought. For a fleeting moment, I enjoy my renegade status. I am a bull in this china shop. Breaking all the rules.

The wedding is one week away. At work, no one has maligned, impugned or fired me. I have not been asked to wear the letter A around the school hallways. I begin to exhale.

One of my students asks to speak to me privately out in the hall. Smart and mouthy, she is working hard to get rid of her old reputation as a teacher's pet. She's wearing black eyeliner; a layer of powdery foundation covers her freckles.

"Are you pregnant?" she whispers, leaning in close, wanting to be supportive in a scarily precocious way.

Caught, flustered, I stammer some response about how inappropriate this is. How a thirteen-year-old should mind her own business.

"I was an accident," she says matter-of-factly. "I wanted you to know."

Later that day, I am sitting on a stool in my classroom watching student presentations. I am wearing a purple Au Coton sweatsuit, mercifully stretchy, with a scarf draped artistically over telltale bulges. My back aches. I shift and rebalance, review last-minute wedding details in my head: Flower pickup. Wine drop-off. Cheque for the string quartet.

I feel this strange sensation inside my belly. Tingles like pins and needles. Flutters like butterfly wings. The accident has spoken.

For the first time in weeks, I laugh.

◇ ◇ ◇

WE GOT MARRIED on a windy, snowy February night. Wedding guests came from near and far.

My parents walked me up the short aisle to the altar, where my husband-to-be stood, nervously, beside his best man. My mom did the first reading, his mom the second— their voices strong and confident. The priest joked that these mothers could probably do the entire Mass without him. We said our vows, signed the register, and returned down the aisle to Bach's "Jesu, Joy of Man's Desiring."

But here was the real magic. Earlier that day, the shop teacher and custodian from my school had met at the church. They set up their ladders and strung tiny white lights overhead. They draped banners of winter white and soft pink over grey panel walls. While cigarette smoke and voices from the AA meeting beyond the partition wafted around them, these two men in their forties, fathers of daughters themselves, transformed the ATCO trailer.

In my thousand and one stories of fairy-tale weddings, this is the story that saved me.

{ **SIX** }

THREE MONTHS LATER, I move away from Calgary, leaving family and friendships behind.

We newlyweds settle into a nice townhouse with rose-coloured curtains. We stack boxes of wedding china and crystal in the upstairs closet. We assemble the new Storkcraft crib and IKEA change table. I take my pregnant body for walks through lonely new suburbs on spring afternoons.

Be grateful. You could be in a wheelchair.

The baby arrives a month early, during one of my frequent trips back to Calgary. Late afternoon in my parents' guestroom bed, I feel what could only be my water breaking. My mother is there to witness and assist. My father drives us to the Grace Hospital across the city. I sit in the front passenger seat on a vinyl tablecloth grabbed from the picnic table. I want to scream when he stops for a yellow light.

"These things don't tend to happen right away," Dad says. (I know for a fact he glued his socks into his shoes to save time getting my mother to the hospital before my sister Kim was born.) Mom tut-tuts from the back seat, reaching forward to pat my shoulder.

The players are all wrong in this drama.

Within a few hours, my husband arrives with a teddy bear and the rolling pin recommended in prenatal classes. Labour is induced. Syntocinon picks up where my body leaves off. I push through darkness into daylight. My doctor—skirt on backwards in her early morning rush to the hospital—consults with the obstetrician on call, his hair on end, roused from his nap in the doctors' lounge. They move into action. Another needle. Long and scary. High and inside. I hear the clanking of stainless-steel forceps that look like giant salad tongs. One tug and the baby pops out. Whimpering and bluish, he is placed on my chest for a moment, then whisked away to the intensive-care nursery. I watch the surgeon press again and again on my belly to make me stop bleeding. He stitches me back together pulling long black thread in and out.

You would have made a good Brownie, I want to tell him.

Small talk from my giddy world of Demerol, exhaustion and relief.

We did it.

◬ ◬ ◬

THIS IS ONE of our first breastfeeding sessions in the neonatal nursery. I am getting the hang of things and relax a little when baby Robert, sleepy from jaundice and preemie jet lag, achieves "latch" with the nurse's assistance. She leaves us on our own in the sitting room. A young woman, no more than twenty, joins me to give her baby a bottle. (A bottle!)

"It's a boy. Nine pounds eight ounces," she says and we exchange labour stories. Twelve hours for me. Two for her.

"I've named him Jonathon." She gazes into his eyes, blue and wide, above the bottle. Big tears drop onto the receiving blanket. "I'm giving him up for adoption," she says quietly. Everything had been arranged. The couple seemed nice. Stable. "I can't give him the kind of life I want him to have."

I hold my baby a little tighter.

Together in the hospital, the baby and I listened to nighttime rains and booming thunder. We shared the first light of morning. Felt afternoon sun warm against our skin. Everything seemed new and wondrous. Any new-mom anxieties could be smoothed away by a ministry of nurses. Safe in that hospital womb, I could stay inside one moment without worrying about the next.

A few days later, my mother drives us home from the hospital. "Things have worked out very well," she tells me.

I agree.

When I try to remember those first few weeks of parenthood, they are a blur. Photos bring them instantly back into focus. There is one of me fast asleep on the bed, arm flung above my head, T-shirt up, breast out, baby sleeping beside me, his little arm flung above his head. I think that was the afternoon the Welcome Wagon lady dropped by. The doorbell rang insistently, incessantly, until we finally answered, roused from our family survival nap upstairs. She swooped in with her basket of goodies, sat in the living room and chatted amiably to this wild-haired zombie couple in terry cloth robes on the couch. Besides the Welcome Wagon, there was a steady stream of relatives and friends dropping in with gifts and well-intentioned advice that sometimes rankled. "Does your baby *really* need a soother?"

Gradually, the three of us got to know each other through a summer of interrupted nights and late-morning sleep-ins. On sunny afternoons, we would go to the swimming pool or beach, the baby squinting and sneezing in the sun between blankets tented over his car seat. We bought a bright yellow bike trailer designed for toddlers to sit upright. Since the car seat didn't fit, we drilled new holes for the nylon straps, laid the baby down flat on a bed of foam and blankets and cinched him in. He seemed to enjoy the ride, looking up at treetops, blue skies and clouds as we trundled along the paths.

We'd always maintained (before having a baby) that having a baby would not stop us from doing things we'd always enjoyed, like cycling, hiking and travelling. We planned to go camping that summer in the Okanagan like we always had. The baby was not going to change things.

On August 16, we loaded up the car with our two-man tent, sleeping bags and camping gear, and set out for the late summer warmth of BC. I know the date simply because it is written on the back of this photo: my husband, in his neon-orange flip-flops and blue anorak, holds the baby on a blizzard-obscured viewpoint on the Jasper-Banff Parkway. Baby's first snowfall.

That would be the high point of the holiday. It was unseasonably cool in the Okanagan Valley—too cold to tent—so we stayed at a motel that smelled of disinfectant soap and old rug. The baby cried nonstop through the night. Nerves frazzled, my husband and I argued in loud whispers, afraid of disturbing the other guests, embarrassed by our parental incompetence. The next day, I spotted my husband's parents strolling hand in hand along the beach where they were camping in the relative warmth and comfort of their travel van. I was giddy with relief. They offered to babysit for the evening so we could go out for dinner on our own. For them, the baby slept peacefully. The next morning, refreshed and restored, we drove all the way back home.

Then came autumn and the return of school. For everyone else. This was the first September since I was five that I wasn't going to school. I was going to be a stay-at-home mom, like my mother before me.

So I set about creating the married life I'd always imagined: the romance of De Beers diamond ads combined with the homemaking skills of my mother, passed on to me through a reprint of *Kate Aitken's Cook Book*. (The original cookbook, worn and split at the binding, still rests in the archive of Mom's dresser drawer.) On the front cover of my new, revised edition, Mom wrote: "A little bit of Kingsland."

Kate Aitken, doyenne of Canadian homemaking, would take it from there. *Your daughter is launched. Grown up, your daughter is now living her own life. But the foundations that you have laid are firm and solid. From you, her second trade of homemaking has been well and truly learned.*

My third trade, motherhood, hadn't been laid in those particular foundations. While my mom would have relied on the 805 recommendations in *Dr. Spock's Baby and Child Care* (1957 edition, also in the dresser drawer), I followed the more current pedagogy of Penelope Leach, which made perfect sense in the clear light of day.

The baby starts to fuss at the same time each night.

Change. Nurse. Soothe. Rock.

Squall.

I feel the frustration. The tears. Maybe I'm no good at this.

Calmly, my husband takes the baby and rocks him in a sliver of moonlight.

"Why won't he go to sleep?" I hate that helpless panic in my voice. "Is he sick? Is he teething?"

"I don't know. He hasn't told me." The rocking chair creaks back and forth, back and forth.

He has always been good with babies.

△ △ △

MY KITCHEN FLOOR became a kind of barometer of how well I was coping with my three new trades. It was sticky and blotched with Rorschach-like spills, begging interpretation. My mother-in-law cheerfully mopped the floor during visits, commenting on the stacks of old newspapers and mounds of white plastic grocery bags that blocked the back stairway. (I was trying to be environmentally responsible *and* creative. I'd read somewhere that you could use plastic bags to stuff cushions for patio furniture.)

My husband likes to be organized. I'd always sensed this but had never lived with it up close. He makes timelines and sets deadlines. Tapes lists of goals on the bathroom mirror. Measures the quality of the day against the list, curling in the steam of morning showers.

I am sleeping in. Again.

Kate Aitken would never have slept in.

Note to Brides: Served for breakfast on a chilly morning, these muffins send any husband whistling off to work.

He switches on the iron to press a shirt. The *tick-tick-tick* of heating metal wakes me up. Angry, defensive.

The laundry basket is heaped high with his shirts, wrinkling daily. I tried my mother's trick of keeping them damp and rolled up in the fridge. Brown mildew seeped around the edges.

My mother made to-do lists on the back of church envelopes—each task written in her determined cursive, stroked through upon completion. Since Mom gave her *Sacrificial Offering to God* in an efficient once-a-month lump sum, there were plenty of envelopes left over. Nearly a year of Sundays and Holy Days of Obligation could be co-opted for lists.

(I recall my own sense of betrayal when I realized that my weekly contribution of a nickel, sometimes my whole dime of allowance, did not go to poor starving people in a far-off country. It got no further than the church sacristy, where I could hear the baskets of loose change being dumped after Mass by the ushers in dark suits.)

Maybe I should make a list.

1. WASH FLOOR

My mom always scrubbed her kitchen floor on hands and knees with an old satin cushion for support, bending herself in the face of bigger priorities—not unlike her prayer. The lino would be stripped with nostril-burning ammonia, then waxed with space-age Aerowax. While she waited for this to dry, she would flip the kitchen chairs upside down on the table, slicing the dirt from each rubber-tipped leg with a paring knife. Cleansing rituals.

On a Thursday afternoon such as this my mother would have scrubbed and waxed or—because it was a blue-sky warm October gift of a day—she might have raked dead leaves into neat piles with brisk, no-nonsense strokes. At night she would have shown me the blisters.

I remember autumn afternoons with Karen's family—how they weren't about work. We picked rose hips near the Glenmore Reservoir in tall grass that smelled like sun.

Quit thinking so much. Make a list.

2. IRON SHIRTS

3. BAKE MUFFINS

With the first skiff of November snow, I began, like generations of women before me, to mobilize for Christmas. I moved into an Arts and Crafts Period that astounded me—given the formative fiasco of my Toymaker's badge.

I commandeered the spare room for my handicraft headquarters, strapping Robert into his Jolly Jumper airplane in the doorway. As he bounced and twirled, I stitched

Christmas stockings and tiny tree decorations on my moth-balled sewing machine, recently recommissioned for the Christmas campaign.

I stockpiled the latest in craft supplies. Glue guns. Fibre-fill. Canisters of liquid embroidery. I recruited the help of my handiest friends. We made puffy fabric-covered photo albums edged in lace. We wrapped plastic margarine containers in calico trimmed with eyelet and presto! Christmas gift baskets with a half-life of two hundred years.

I baked enough goodies to feed an army, whipping butter and icing sugar until my avocado-green Sunbeam mixer smelled like burning rubber. I field-tested recipes featured on *Canada* A M along with the old-fashioned favourites from my mom and Kate: Melting Moments, Nan's Shortbread, Walnut Drops.

Note to Gourmets: These cookies are rich, delectable and highly popular. Serve at your top-drawer parties or when entertaining your mother-in-law.

And there was shopping to do.

Manoeuvres to the malls for baby bestsellers like *Goodnight Moon* and toys recommended by the Canadian Toy Testing Council. Convoys to Calgary for just the right clothing: designer denim overalls for the photo with Santa, festive plaid pajamas to wear on Christmas morning.

The Christmas campaign was a total success, judging from the photographs. In three separate houses in three separate cities, we celebrated baby's first Christmas.

January swirled in. Cold. Snowy. Aimless.

Make a list.

1. PAY BILLS AT CANADA TRUST

2. PICK UP PHOTOS AT LONDON DRUGS

3. UPDATE BABY BOOK

I was bound and determined to keep this baby book up to date. I'd discovered my own baby book—totally blank—in Mom's dresser drawer when I was thirteen. I'd written a scathing note inside the front cover: "Since I was the last baby born, my baby book remains empty. So this book will pass on to my offspring, if any. Let us hope I can succeed in filling this in, where my mother failed." My mother had returned the book to me shortly after Robert was born, smirking as she threw down the gauntlet.

4. CLEAN BATHROOMS

5. VACUUM

My mother actually enjoyed vacuuming. Three phases of fashionable floor coverings: wool area rugs, wall-to-wall sculptured broadloom and an unforgettable white Orlon shag (which she also raked) had been sucked into submission by three different vacuum cleaners: the Lewyt, the Kirby and the Fantom. After the rugs had been vacuumed (or the oven scoured, or the freezer scraped free of frost) Mom would use her remaining time to work on a project. Home decorating, typically, but something that could be divided into productive blocks and frequent errands to Woodward's for paint, wallpaper or MACtac.

Maybe I need a project.

It took me two weeks to paint four wooden chairs. Paintbrushes soaking in pickle jars of turpentine congealed into chunks of green bristle.

Home decorating projects. Self-preservation in turpentine brine.

I tried sewing something instead: a baby activity book made of red, yellow and blue cloth with an assortment of buttons, grommets, Velcro and zippers that would have my child dressing himself in no time. He would also learn his colours, numbers and letters.

I would never have considered myself a great seamstress, since I lacked the most important quality: patience. My most memorable junior high sewing project was a culotte-halter-jumpsuit made in a jaunty nautical print. I ditched all the instructions about ironing seams and clipping curves, determined to sew it within the ninety minutes promised on the Simplicity pattern envelope: "Make it tonight! Wear it tomorrow!"

Near midnight, I stepped triumphantly into the culottes, reached through my legs to grab the front section and tie the lumpy straps around my neck. The seams were puckered and crooked. Entire sections were held together by loops of hand sewing where I couldn't bother to figure out the concept of facings. Still, I wore it to school the next day, feeling what my mother must have meant when she described someone as frumpy.

(My mother could not rescue me in the sewing department; her experience was confined to dead-straight seams on curtains and pleater tape.)

I threw my nautical number in the neighbour's garbage can.

I didn't sew again until high school when I worked part-time in a fabric store. Now, here were women who knew the value of virgin wool Viyella and the potential of polyester crepe. They could wrestle sixty-inch bolts of fabric onto display racks and drape them *just so*. And wow, could they topstitch! Under their tutelage—and tendency to check for finished seams and neat hems—my sewing improved.

I was the youngest sales clerk—definitely the least motivated to straighten, tidy and drape—so I spent a lot of time looking through pattern books and chatting with my co-workers. Most of them worked part-time, too; their full-time jobs were being wives and mothers to children at various ages and stages. I loved to hear the stories from three generations of women.

There was the short, energetic Ada, who still made homemade cookies for her two grown kids and prattled on hopefully about engagements and weddings. There was Vivian, the wise and witty grandmother, who told me, when I tried to take another Saturday off, "Either work or gad. You can't do both."

Gad?

(*To go about idly or in search of pleasure.*)

My favourite was Cheryl, tall, blond and regal. She had the married life I planned on having. A hardworking, sensitive husband with a sense of humour. Three adorable blond children. Tidy, tasteful house with handmade quilts, homemade bread and a dog.

We became good friends. Later she would tell me that her need to be perfect early in her marriage made her so sick that she needed to be hospitalized.

I think of her now as I make my list, looking out on leaden February skies.

1. BAKE COOKIES
2. DO LAUNDRY
3. ORGANIZE LINEN CLOSET
4. SEW VELCRO TABS ON BABY'S ACTIVITY BOOK

I hate writing these fucking lists.
I want to write other things instead.

◊ ◊ ◊

IT IS ANOTHER *cold grey morning. Cars line the street outside the daycare to unload their little human cargoes, complete with snowsuits and backpacks. Organized children, organized parents begin their carefully scheduled days.*

She watches the scene from the front window, where her day has also begun. Husband at work, baby back to sleep, she considers her plans for the day. Pulling the thinning terry robe up around her knees, she balances her third cup of lukewarm, over-steeped tea. This feels like Saturday mornings used to, but less deserved. It's only Tuesday.

Outside, the daycare rush subsides and the world slips into quiet routine. Everyone is at work or school or home. The piano strains of Peter Gzowski's Morningside *remind her that it is now after nine and she should be doing something productive. Breakfast dishes? Laundry? Shower? Then what? She feels a little panicked—a familiar uncertainty about how to shape her day. How to defend herself from the envy she feels when her husband returns from his workday textured with deadlines nailed and missions accomplished, asking, "What did you do today?"*

She'd always imagined in her work-weary other life that staying at home would be easy. At first, her days were one giant to-do list with long- and short-term goals. Everything from the mundane: mop the floor, to the erudite: read Madame Bovary. *And there was that perma-goal of getting her postpartum body back into shape.*

But now she wants more noteworthy projects. Bigger reasons to shed the housecoat early and work diligently while baby sleeps. Like those success profiles in the women's magazines she now has time to read. She could be like Lynn Johnston creating a comic strip from her everyday experiences. Maybe she could write for magazines like Hope, the stay-at-home mom on TV's *thirty-something who explored, weekly, their shared world of identity anxieties, but with perfect hair and clothes to die for.*

The baby's cry suddenly limits her choices. Relieved, she moves into action. Drains the dregs of cold tea. Runs up the stairs. Baby's goals for the day are packed into just this moment. She can disappear into them.

◇ ◇ ◇

I PLANT A VEGETABLE GARDEN in spring. Seed Grand Rapids lettuce, Nantes carrots, sugar snap peas, yellow bush beans and butternut squash. Tamp. Water. Wait.

Tentative green shoots appear a few weeks later in crooked, self-conscious rows. I am proud, empowered. Quackgrass, chickweed, Russian thistles spring up. Uninvited guests at my garden party.

"You've got to keep those weeds down," my father-in-law warns. A seasoned gardener, he orders from seed catalogues each winter. Plants tomatoes in peat moss containers at Easter. Transplants on the long weekend in May. Waters and weeds religiously through hot, dry southern Alberta summers.

Note to Brides: If you have never canned, pickled or preserved, you will find the whole procedure highly rewarding.

In August, I pick my prodigious vegetable harvest. Submerge peas, beans and carrots in boiling water. Plunge them into ice.

The whole procedure is highly exhausting.

Ziploc bags of vegetables will languish for months at the bottom of the deep-freeze. Ice-bound relics of an ill-fated expedition in search of some mythic passage.

"You planted too much in the garden," my husband says.

Note to Brides: Standing at the top of the cellar stairs, drop the squash firmly on the cement floor below. This method never fails nor does it cut the fingers. One word of warning: Make certain your new husband is not at the bottom of the cellar steps.

I returned to teaching that September. Another attempt at self-preservation using an earlier version of myself: energetic, creative teacher with great clothes and excellent shoes who writes plays and plans pep rallies. I thought teaching would deliver me from the restlessness of being at home.

It is the night of parent-teacher interviews. I am sitting on a metal folding chair at my trapezoid-shaped table in the gymnasium. "Ms. Campbell: Language Arts&Drama" reads the dot-matrix computer banner taped on the wall behind me. I am wearing my ultramarine-blue power suit with a pin-striped silk shirt and matching blue pumps. I straighten my sheaf of papers and smile pleasantly at the parents sitting opposite.

I feel a sudden cramp in my gut and a warning swirl from stomach to esophagus to throat. I bolt, in three-inch heels, across the gym floor to the girls washroom and throw up, violently, splattering suit, shirt and shoes in the process. A second wave—diarrhea this time—leaves me slumped over in the washroom cubicle, panting, sweating, panicking.

My husband drives me to the hospital. By this time, my body is covered in hives. Face puffy, eyes swollen shut. The nurse gives me a shot of epinephrine. I begin to shake uncontrollably beneath the warm flannel sheet.

What's wrong with me?

The food poisoning theory is ruled out when the whole thing happens again a month later. And the month after that.

"It's an allergic reaction," says my doctor, who assures me these things can and do develop in adults—even ones with allergy-free, stable childhoods.

What could I possibly be allergic to? Chalk dust? Mould circulating through school air ducts?

"This could be a reaction to stress," the specialist in Calgary hypothesizes. "This seems to happen around the same time each month when your body is more vulnerable."

Stress with a PMS chaser?

Okay, I admit it. Marriage is tough. Those disagreements about whose turn it is to cook, who gets up for the baby at night, who calls in sick to work when the baby gets sick, whose teaching job is more demanding. There seems to be no time for a relationship between baby, work, meals and a house that never stays clean.

Okay, I admit it. A little part of me has begun to resent teaching. The same old routine, the planning, the marking. Maybe I want a little more time with my own child instead of everyone else's—although he is thriving at a dayhome with playmates, play dough and a wonderful caregiver. My husband is thriving at a new school with interesting, fun, generally athletic colleagues. By association, I should be thriving. But I'm not.

⌂ ⌂ ⌂

IT IS A COLD NIGHT in February. Snow, illuminated by streetlights, falls gently and melts on the windshield. I sit in my car, watching, waiting for the lights in the office building to snap on, the lobby doors to swing wide open.

This is my first visit to this psychologist. I've heard that he is understanding and wise.

"Tell me what brings you here."

This feels like Confession used to, but more forgiving.

"It has been ten years since my last counselling session. These are my issues: I get sick a lot. I am never happy. And I used to be fun."

The psychologist asks about my marriage. Sounds perfectly normal when I lay it out like this. Nice husband, nice child, nice house.

The problem is me.

He asks about my job. I like teaching, but it's busy. I tell him I was grading drama exams while I waited outside in the car.

"Drama *exams*?" he repeats.

He asks about my health. I cite allergies, stomach pains, fatigue.

"That's called somaticizing," he tells me. "Your body does the admitting for you."

He asks about my life before I moved from Calgary. I tell him the stories of growing up, my connection to Mom, how we both loved shopping.

"I really miss Chinook Centre." The laugh catches in my throat.

He paces in front of the black leather sectional. Pauses. "You don't mind if I pace?"

I shake my head.

He continues. Stop. Go. Syncopated thought. Freud, Skinner and Erikson argue in the Gentlemen's Club of his brain.

I stare at the rocks, polished smooth, on the coffee table.

"Could you," he asks me a few sessions later, "set aside some time each day to sit alone and think? Try some creative visualization—imagine things that you'd like to do. Not the *shoulds*. The *coulds*."

Permission. The Etch-a-Sketch turned upside down and shaken.

I keep track of my thoughts and ideas in a yellow chintz-bound journal, a long-ago birthday gift from my mother.

Inside, I am free to admit disappointments and play with possibilities.

{ SEVEN }

THE SCHOOL YEAR finally ends. We collapse into summer. Skirmishes on the home front subside. My husband mows the lawn. I tend the garden. We both paint the fence. We have a successful family camping holiday in BC. We even manage to get away for a few days on our own, leaving Robert in the capable hands of my mother, "Gran," who has bought a sandbox and wading pool and planned a week's worth of outings and excursions on her calendar.

We agree on one thing: it is time to have a second child. Sex resumes with this shared purpose. This time, a pink home pregnancy test confirms the result. Any wisps of ambivalence about the relationship or teaching are dispelled into the biosphere of my pregnant self. Even the allergies disappear.

With no wedding to rush or reputation to save, I can experience pregnancy on its own terms. There's the usual tiredness and morning sickness between routine visits to the doctor, where I read Robert, now three, the lost puppy storybook over and over. He gets a sticker when my finger gets poked for blood. I see the baby on ultrasound. Hear the heart on the Doppler monitor whoosh like a skipping rope on "pepper." These are the moments that I missed the first time around.

Our second son, Michael, is born October 30, the same day of the Clearblue test four years earlier when my life took a sharp detour. This seems to set things straight. My life is back on track.

I'm actually happy to be at home with my kids, who become friends, despite Robert's initial plea to take the baby—squalling and red-faced—back to the hospital. Everyone settles into a routine.

My days are now spent driving to Jazzercise, the donut shop, the children's library or the mall. We go to swimming lessons, gymnastics and preschool programs. There are playdates at plastic-tunnelled labyrinths named Moonwalkers, birthdays at McDonald's and "mother's time out" discussion groups. I perambulate through this daytime world with other stay-at-home moms—most of whom seem to get up earlier than me to put on makeup and style their hair. They have great clothes and excellent shoes. They seem completely content in this world.

Little by little, my restlessness returns. I knew it would.

I wish my mother was here to coach me through this. She hasn't been able to visit for a while. In the five years since her retirement, she has suffered a series of mishaps in the most benign of circumstances. She tore ankle ligaments while stepping off the back porch. Her retina detached while she swam laps at the YMCA. She slipped on a shampoo spill and wrenched her back at The Bay. She tripped on a carpet and broke her hip at Safeway. Errands—the hallmark of her busy life—have become perilous.

I remember our last visit to Calgary after her hip surgery. She had just come home from the hospital and was resting in her bedroom. She was in agonizing pain but didn't tell anyone. She asked for tea instead.

I remember my silent fury because she couldn't get up to play with her grandsons—whom I had primed all week for this visit. I wanted to stamp my feet, shout at her to get out of bed, help me feel good about my life.

Suddenly, I see myself at four years old in the same hallway. Sunlight streams through the window and warms the floor where I sit, doing a puzzle. All by myself. Big chunky pieces of cardboard will make a doll with fuzzy-wuzzy yellow hair. My mom has taught me how to look for the shapes and colours that match. I try, at first, to do that. But there are too many pieces. None of them fit together the way they should. My fingers bend the cardboard edge, try to coax it into place. My fingers curl into a fist, pounding the puzzle piece again and again.

I am thirty-four years old, still feeling the helpless frustration of that child.

Later, I am unnerved by the number of prescription bottles I see in Mom's bathroom medicine cabinet. Morphine sulphate, Oxycocet and Rhovane line the shelves where the iodine and Band-Aids used to be.

My mother is in chronic pain.

I have to learn to cope without her.

◊ ◊ ◊

ONE NIGHT A WEEK, I head out to a magazine writing course at the community college. Tentatively, hopefully, I mail out my first request for article submission guidelines to *Canadian Living* magazine. It takes me three hours and ten botched envelopes to figure out the block format on my computer. It is a personal victory when the guidelines arrive in my Self Addressed Stamped Envelope. I buy a book called *Magazine Writing from the Boonies,* which I read cover to cover at the dentist's office. I brainstorm ideas for magazine articles while in the bathtub, drinking Grand Marnier. Every Thursday afternoon, I take my kids to the babysitter so I can write, undisturbed, at home. On Saturday mornings, I leave home to write at the donut shop. A table of one's own.

◊ ◊ ◊

HER WHITE VOLKSWAGEN GOLF *is parked out on the driveway, frozen solid even though the winter has been mild. There is a gaping hole in the front grill of the car where the identifying* VW *monogram used to be. There's a side-door dent from a close encounter with a flagpole. Rust spots re-emerge from behind peeling touch-up paint.*

A huge orange tow truck chugs up alongside the car. The driver perfunctorily pops the hood and zaps the dead battery with so many volts of surrogate energy. He blasts off in a plume of white exhaust, leaving the little Volkswagen sputtering toward a rough, tentative idle.

"I'm feeling a lot like my car these days," she says as she watches the rescue through her living room window. Grey streaks of hair re-emerge beneath fading highlights. Assorted dings and dents from two children. Gaping hole where her personality used to be. She imagines the bright orange truck screeching back from the corner, careering into her living room, stopping just short of the patio doors. Out jumps the cable-toting guy in a jumpsuit, smelling not unpleasantly of garages and gasoline. He walks toward her and clamps a giant red jaw onto her cranium. The black jaw grips the floral chintz footstool to ground the connection. "Start her up!"

☐ ☐ ☐

IN SEPTEMBER, I returned to full-time teaching. With a mortgage and a new minivan, we needed the money. This time, the excitement of *real* writing sustained me. While my students worked on their stories and poems, I wrote leads for article proposals: How to foster family literacy. How to handle Christmas stress. At the public library, I skimmed through back issues of magazines, copying information from the mastheads of *Chatelaine, Homemakers, Today's Parent*. Some nights, after the kids were in bed, I'd go back to school to use the secretary's new colour computer and laser printer. I'd mail my queries from the same postal outlet for good luck.

Finally, it happened. My first article was published. One hundred words in an American trade magazine for librarians.

I got business cards printed: Freelance Writer.

At night in bed, I'd keep us both awake with plans, my words spilling out in a hopeful torrent.

"Maybe we could spend this summer at a cabin somewhere like the Gulf Islands. Maybe I could write in the morning while you take care of the kids and we could do family things together in the afternoon. Maybe I could teach part-time and write..."

He responds sleepily from some far-off shore, "What do I get to do?"

I am alone and adrift, miles of ocean between us.

△ △ △

SALT.

That was the topic of the sermon at our wedding. "Salt preserves, salt seasons," the priest began in his rumbling, rambling voice of a thousand sermons. Salty tales from an old salt. Take it with a grain of salt. What was his point about salt and marriage anyway? Was it from the New

Testament parable—you are the salt of the earth: honest, faithful, loyal—or a cautionary tale from the Old Testament? Lot's wife. Turned to a pillar of salt when she disobeyed and looked back. Wife's lot.

I kept on writing, knowing the time I spent alone was straining our relationship. Sarcastic and critical exchanges began to corrode the marriage.

Finally, I hit the wall.

Actually, a Little Tikes toy drum hit the wall because I'd thrown it there as hard as I could. I'd also kicked the bathroom door and smashed a dinner plate on the kitchen floor.

"You're crazy!"

I sank down onto the carpet and curled up on my side. I heard the same gut-wrenching, heart-breaking sobs of my mother all those years ago.

Everything I do fails.

My children watched wide-eyed and silent.

△ △ △

"IT'S NOT AS THOUGH she's going to take the family fortune and go write in the mountains of Colombia."

This is my psychologist speaking. Trying to lighten the mood of this first counselling session. For couples. My dream sounds so normal—not crazy, not selfish—when he lays it out like this.

"She wants to be a writer."

I wrote my very first story in grade three for my favourite teacher, Miss MacNeil. It was printed neatly in pencil on long foolscap sheets with words like *delighted, astonished* and *flabbergasted*. I lay in bed at night thinking up names for my characters. Granny Biddle. Mr. Chubbletooth. At the end of the year, my teacher gave me a red *Winston Canadian Dictionary*. On the inside cover, she had written in magical turquoise ink: "This may be some help to an author. Good Luck in your writing."

I was hooked. Stories and skits in elementary school evolved, with more encouragement from teachers, into essays and plays and the high school newspaper. I'd never lost my desire to be a writer. Just my youthful certainty.

△ △ △

"YOU HAVE A MESSAGE on your answering machine," my mother-in-law tells me when I get home from school. She has come to help with our children's chain run of chicken-pox during an especially bleak and cold January. "Someone in Toronto. Something about a magazine." Heart racing, hands shaking, I play back the message: "We want to pub-lish your article." I hit rewind. Listen again. And again. I phone my sisters and make them listen. My first full-length feature article, 2,500 words conceived and crafted here in the boonies, is going to be published in a major Canadian magazine.

The edition came out that spring, my article title in bold white letters on the glossy cover. A few weeks later, I got a card in the mail. Even before I opened it, I knew it was from Miss MacNeil. I recognized the ink.

△ △ △

I POUR ANOTHER CUP of tea and head downstairs to my basement office—an IKEA pine tabletop on trestles, a metal folding chair and a dhurrie rug on the cold cement floor. On the desk is my brand new Macintosh Performa 640 computer. Lightning fast at 33 MHZ with 8 MB of RAM, a 500 MB hard drive and an impressive 18-inch colour monitor. I assemble my writing tools: spiral steno book of interview notes, yellow newsprint pad of fledgling drafts handwritten in blue BIC microtip. I switch on the computer and wait for the start-up theme that sounds like "ta-da!"

I am working on my third feature article for this magazine. "How your relationship as a couple is a role model for your children." I didn't know whether to laugh or cry when my editor assigned it.

I've finished a few telephone interviews with parenting experts. I've done the cross-Canada checkup on how couples get along after kids come along. Whitehorse, Calgary, Toronto, Halifax. I can't get this one family out of my mind. The couple had divorced several years earlier but continued to raise their son together—apart—by alternating weeks. Their son, now twelve, sounded okay with it. He was well-spoken. Seemed well-adjusted.

Could I be a single parent?

The movies roll in my mind.

SCENE 1

She is sitting with her mother at the donut shop—or some tonier spot. There is the usual chit-chat about children, teaching and adventures in home decorating. She drops the bomb: "I'm leaving my marriage."

Her mother crumples into her cruller.

"Couldn't you just wallpaper instead?"

SCENE 2

Christmas. His family will gather around the table with plates heaped high with turkey, mashed potatoes with gravy and dressing—her favourite. There will be grandparents, uncles, aunts, cousins, nieces and nephews sharing stories, jokes and easy laughter. There will be walks in the wintry air or ice-skating on the community rink. She won't be there.

The in-law has become the outlaw.

SCENE 3

She lives in a basement suite in a rundown apartment block with no backyard on a busy street. Two boys in torn jean jackets sit on the curb smoking, swearing and drinking Slurpees. The children of divorce...

A lawn mower roars by the basement window, flinging clods of dirt against the glass. My mind movies end. Who am I kidding? I could never manage things on my own. I can't even mow the lawn.

Our counselling sessions continue. Differences are discussed. Strategies are suggested. "Maybe some time apart would help both of you choose to be together."

"Or maybe we're just not trying hard enough."

We plan a family summer holiday. Time to try harder.

We rent a cabin in the Gulf Islands for a week. We spend entire days at the seashore with the kids, canoeing along the shoreline, our Prairie kids pointing and gasping at purple starfish clinging to rocks. They dig up crabs and clams, squatting beside tide pools, their hair white blond in the August sun. I go for long solitary walks to the Point. I make wishes on spectacular sunsets. Late at night, I write on yellow newsprint sheets about things I don't want to write about.

This happened a few days ago at the Lonsdale Market. We were standing in a long line-up to have balloon creatures made for the kids. The Vancouver rain had driven everyone indoors.

A husband and wife were ahead of us in line. She was leaning on his shoulder, her hand resting gently on his arm. He was cradling their blond baby, who'd fallen asleep. Together, they watched their older son talk to the balloon-maker about his wish for a hat. The mom was smiling, eyes crinkled behind her glasses. It seemed so easy, the sharing of a nice family moment. I wanted to cry—and did, several hours later—in the washroom stall at the McDonald's on Lonsdale Avenue.

I'm crying in washroom stalls again. I know my life is changing.

MESSAGE IN A BOTTLE
Not now
You don't know me
Not now
I don't know you
Not now
The kids will hear us
Not now
I've forgotten how to kiss.

⌂ ⌂ ⌂

IT'S JUST ME with the psychologist now.

"I don't know what to do. I'm scared to stay. Scared to go."

He suggests, gently, that an antidepressant might help me through this.

My physician writes the prescription and gives me a free sample: seven days of Paxil in a starter pack. I am scared to break the seal.

Courage will have to come from someplace else.

⌂ ⌂ ⌂

"DAD HAS HAD a fall."

It is my mother on the phone from Calgary, her voice its usual calm contralto.

"All of a sudden, he slumped against the dishwasher and fell onto the kitchen floor. I knelt down beside him and held his head."

I imagine my mother kneeling—contorting—beside my father midway between the fridge and stove. Her hip replacement is just a few months old.

"He was conscious—but very pale and frightened. We called 9-1-1."

That is a first for my parents. They don't like to make a scene.

"The paramedics took him to the hospital for tests. They were very good with Dad."

She has always called him Dad.

The tests showed nothing unusual.

He has never had this problem before.

It begins with a few restless nights. The dark morning hours are elastic: stretching, stretching, snapping.

What's going on? Why can't I sleep? What's wrong with me?

My dad has insomnia.

No need to worry. Go to bed earlier. Keep up the 5BX Plan from the air force days. Jog a little longer on the mini-trampoline. Try to nap in the afternoon...

Retirement allows for this kind of flexibility. The reward of a carefully managed life.

For twenty-five years, Dad began work at eight o'clock sharp every weekday morning. Dressed in his suit, shirt and tie, he'd head downstairs with a mug of black instant coffee. At nine, he'd go out on sales calls, leaving his telephone answering service to take messages. He'd return at noon and make his lunch: Puritan Meat Spread with hot mustard on brown toast, pickled egg on the side and coffee. Every other week, he would drive to Edmonton, proselytizing about Pyrotenax heating cables: copper wires sheathed in white magnesium oxide that conduct electricity without melting or burning.

"Dad isn't doing too well."

It is my mother on the phone again.

"He's still not sleeping."

This means that she's not either. Her nighttime vigil has resumed.

"Now he's not eating—says he has no appetite."

She says he frets about the oddest things. Whether the car has been tuned up for summer. (It had.) Whether his tax return was sent in. (It was.) Whether all that electrical wiring he'd done years ago in the basement was unsafe.

"Just yesterday, I found him at the fuse box downstairs flicking switches, pulling wires."

My father is burning inside.

∆ ∆ ∆

THIS IS the Holy Cross hospital. The poplars lining the street are gold against a blue September sky. I was born in this old building of brown brick with tall cement pillars.

Robert, six, is eager to visit Granddad in the hospital. As the first grandson, he has experienced the best of my father. Healthy. Robust. Content. When Robert was a baby, Dad would carry him from the backyard to the front, pointing out the tall birch trees and white jet streams up above. "Time for our spiritual walk," he would say.

Dad is sitting in an orange Naugahyde chair beside the bed. He is dressed in his regular clothes—brown pants, checkered long-sleeved shirt, tie and cardigan.

"Hi, Dad. It's good to see you."

He smiles shakily as I bend to kiss him hello. His eyes behind his glasses are magnified, watery and vague. His lips are chapped, dry saliva crusted at the corners of his mouth. The medications do that. But they keep him from fretting—sliding worry after worry across an abacus of fear.

Dad and Robert play checkers. I've never seen my dad play any board game. ("Uninteresting" his usual reaction to card games, small talk or any discussion of feelings.)

Dad used to say he came from the most boring province to draw: Saskatchewan. A long, tall trapezoid, with no Hudson Bay to squiggle around or interesting islands to colour in afterward. Even Alberta had a steep slope in its southwest corner. Perhaps that is why, as a child, Dad looked to the sky for inspiration. Not as in God or heaven—more like airplanes and radio waves. By day, he dreamed of working in the control tower at the Regina Airport. At night, he'd listen to the dance band sounds of Artie Shaw and the Dorsey Brothers in distant hotel ballrooms of America, travelling crystal clear over radio through a starlit Saskatchewan sky.

Dad hasn't played his saxophone in months.

I listen to the snick of checkers moving across the board.

Dad shares this room with a rodeo clown, who is away on a weekend pass. I look for a wig of curly red hair on the nightstand or big shoes under the bed.

The checker game ends. Robert wins. Dad shakes his hand.

"Thanks for the visit."

I hesitate, then remind Dad about my insomnia problem ten years before. How frustrating and frightening it was. How it went away. Eventually.

"How did you get to sleep again?"

I reach into memory for some practical advice. Dale Carnegie-style hints. Feelings are all I can find.

"I had to learn to trust myself. There was this little girl inside me who didn't believe the adult could handle things."

This is not the kind of answer he wants.

This is the only answer I need.

◊ ◊ ◊

I PLANT CROCUS and daffodil bulbs in my garden in late October. Dig them into hard, nearly frozen ground. Cover them gently with soil and leaves.

I will not be here to see them when they bloom in spring.

PART 3

{ EIGHT }

I THREW MY WEDDING dress in a dumpster.

Not out of spite. Not out of anger. It was pure practicality.

The dress had been sliding back and forth in the trunk of my car since I'd left. When the jug of windshield washer fluid tipped, leaking fluorescent pink splotches onto ivory satin, it murdered any chance of that dress reinventing itself in some consignment store.

I planned on reinventing myself.

Completely.

Three months earlier, I had moved out, leaving my marriage of seven years.

The news spread quickly among family, friends, co-workers. When a marriage breaks up, one needs to stake a loyalty claim early.

I told my mother over the phone. She said she was not surprised; I'd broached the subject with her months before. She said "Oh dear" and "Are you sure?" in all the right places but her unspoken message was clear: personal unhappiness is no reason to take apart a marriage.

I asked Mom to tell Dad about the separation, relying on our time-worn triangulation to avoid his judgment and scorn. There had been no suppertime lectures on Divorce. The closest we kids had come to the subject was dressing up in the cast-off evening gowns of a glamorous divorcee neighbour who smoked and drove a white Pontiac convertible. In our family, marriage was a contract—legally and morally binding.

A few days after our phone conversation, my mother sent me a letter full of abstractions about societal pressures and psychological programming. "This is not intended as a mother's homily," she wrote, "but to say, were it possible, I would fix things so the pain and disillusionment would disappear."

I reread the words, her truth told in slanted cursive. Was she apologizing for not being able to run to my rescue—to clear up this latest in a series of fuck-ups? Or was she saying, finally, that she trusted me to figure things out for myself?

"I have to find my own way," I wrote back. "You have no map for this part of the journey."

Neither did I.

△ △ △

WHEN I WAS TEN, I drew a road map of my life with no-nonsense assertions of where I'd been and where I planned to go. A race car, carefully copied from a Matchbox minia-ture, wound around the track past checkered flags marking my birth, Baptism (this was a title page for religion class, after all) grade six, high school graduation and university.

The most impressive feature of this map was an enor-mous diamond ring I'd coloured with my Smoke Grey Laurentian pencil crayon, adding lines to make the diamond look sparkly and a dollar sign to make it look expensive. I wrote "ENGAGED" beside it in big block letters and "MAR-RIED" a respectable car-length away.

My map ended there on the edge of the loose-leaf page.

△ △ △

MY HUSBAND AND I agreed to attend mediation, a new government-funded program for couples to work through their separations and, ideally, avoid adversarial, expensive courtroom battles. Our mediator knew the terrain well, hav-ing been through her own divorce years earlier. She regaled us with stories of just how nasty it could get. After several strained and emotional sessions, we agreed that the boys would spend one week with their dad, one week with their mom. Shared parenting was the new frontier.

Our children were the last to know.

We agonized over when and where and what to tell them. How to gently break their hearts.

It is a bitterly cold Wednesday night in February. I'm helping Robert build his new LEGO pirate ship in the living room. He proceeds methodically, patiently, while I quietly curse the directions.

Later, he sits beside his dad on the couch and I sit close by on the footstool. We both know the phrases we are supposed to use:

"Your dad and I don't love each other enough to live together anymore," followed by:

"This isn't your fault," concluding with:

"We still love you."

Words that couldn't even graze the real story. All those hopeful attempts to get it right.

Robert listens. Nods. Searches for a brave response inside his shy, six-year-old self.

"Michael will miss you too much," he tells me. Big tears roll soundlessly down his cheeks. "Who will help me finish my pirate ship?"

Michael, three, didn't understand. He clung to his blue clown blanket and his dad's leg as he watched me close the door and walk out into darkness. He still holds the memory of that night, along with the blanket, tattered and thin. "I thought you were leaving forever."

Mothers are never supposed to leave.

I was staying at a friend's but needed a place of my own. Our house seemed to belong to him now. He liked the yard and the sunny southern exposure. Staying there would provide some stability for the kids. For me, it was strewn with ghosts of sadder times that no amount of vacuuming could clear.

On a grey Saturday in March, I hired a moving company with big hearts painted on the side of the truck. The movers hauled out some furniture and a stack of boxes—the acquisitions of seven years dispersed in less than two hours and moved into a pink stucco townhouse I'd rented from a divorcee who smoked. It was plunked in a treeless expanse of new suburb where the wind whined through the power lines, swirling dust and snow into gritty grey drifts.

I remember my first night alone in the townhouse.

In the upstairs bedroom, I unrolled a slab of green foam and covered it with my faded floral Marimekko sheets from my first apartment. I crawled under the duvet and waited for sleep to come. Turned from one side to the other. Flipped the pillow to its cool underside. Stared at the light fixture on the ceiling.

What if I can't sleep?

I thought about my kids, our bedtime stories and routines. The silly words we sang to "Mama's gonna buy you a mockingbird." The hundreds of times we read *Are You My Mother?* ("You are not my mother. You are a Snort!") Their warm arms around my neck as I kissed them goodnight. Michael always asked, "Can you tickle my feet?"

Maybe this was all a big mistake. Maybe I should get up, drive the five blocks back home, sneak in the front door, lie down on the living room couch, wake up to the life I left.

Just come home to sleep.

My mother's advice from years before haunts me.

I'm not sure where home is anymore.

The next day, I set up my desk and computer in the mint-green living room. Lacking a couch, I scattered a few cushions on the rug in an Arabian Nights style, like the inside of the bottle on *I Dream of Jeannie*. My floral chintz chair—originally my father's brown armchair—I arranged kitty-corner beside a dying fig tree. In the kitchen, a stack of cardboard U-Haul boxes waited to be unpacked and organized into cupboards.

They never were. I never really moved into that pink townhouse completely, although I had no trouble sleeping there. (Maybe I could get night rates.) It would become my halfway house. A place to gather the threads of a life I'd ripped apart.

△ △ △

APRIL.

Easter dinner with my parents in Calgary. Just the kids and me.

"I'm in mourning," my father announces over the Brussels sprouts. Says he misses the suppertime discussions with his son-in-law. Politics. Science. Religion.

Any ground I'd gained in my lifelong struggle for Dad's approval is suddenly under siege.

"I know you don't like me!" he fires off. "Maybe you just don't like men."

"That's not true," I protest. "That's not why I left."

"Why *did* you leave, then?"

I can't answer that. Not in a rational way that would make sense to him.

"It's hard to explain."

He hesitates. Reloads.

"Do you know how this divorce is going to affect your children?"

"No, Dad, I don't."

"I just hope you've learned from your mistakes."

That is his parting shot.

For weeks afterward, I fumed. So what was I supposed to have learned? And what, exactly, were my mistakes? Getting divorced? Getting married? Getting pregnant? Being born?—that pesky Midge-mistake in the first place?

What about *his* mistakes?

I replayed our dinner conversation over and over again until it sounded like one of those debates my father so missed and mourned.

Resolved: That my father was emotionally unavailable in my formative years, which caused damage to my self-esteem.

I would open my argument with a quote from Dr. Spock's *Baby and Child Care,* 1957 edition.

A girl needs a friendly father, too. She gains confidence in herself as a girl and a woman from feeling his approval.

"You were unaffectionate. You never cuddled or hugged. You rarely kissed us goodnight."

Dad would rebut this by blaming his own mother, who had coddled him, keeping him in long blond curls and short pants until grade one. He was simply not the affectionate type.

"You never told me you loved me."

Dad would argue that he *showed* rather than told. Didn't he build us an amazing backyard with a sandbox and swing set? Didn't he teach me to drive and change a flat tire?

"You were distant and aloof. You never knew my hopes and fears."

Actually, this point would be moot. Mom was the warden of my emotional frontier; Dad would never trespass.

Somewhere in my early teens, I had made a conscious effort to improve my relationship with Dad, to strengthen that father-daughter bond.

I didn't have many routines or resources to work with. Like most fathers of the era, Dad relegated himself to household infrastructure. He went to work, mowed the lawn and did all the highway driving, his portable heater and snow chains stored in the trunk, just in case.

He *did* watch a few of my softball games and dutifully attended Christmas concerts and piano recitals. Sometimes, we took the dog for long car rides in the country, the conversation flagging when Haggis fell asleep on the floor between us.

Dad loved his import cars. I tried to be loyal to his purchases of Rovers and Peugeots but really wished he would buy a Ford station wagon with jump seats that flipped up in the back.

Dad loved his music. He played in a combo band called the Nova Tones that played weekend nights at the Legion or Elks. My classical piano training left Dad more perplexed than proud.

"Can't you play by ear?" he would ask, clipping his alto saxophone onto his neck strap and leafing through his sheet music of handwritten melody lines. "Can't you just add in the bass chords?"

My demure "Polonaise" didn't stand a chance against "Five Foot Two, Eyes of Blue" played with a rollicking, ham-fisted bass.

It was cable television that, ultimately, hooked us up. Saturday evenings at six o'clock would find my dad and me in our basement rumpus room, watching the new offerings of syndicated American TV shows transmitted from KXLY in Spokane, Washington. Our evening's entertainment began with the pompadoured Porter Wagoner singing "Her and the Car and the Mobile Home Was Gone" with an even-bigger-haired, buxom songbird of Tennessee named Dolly Parton. We laughed at their sequined suits. But the main event of our musical evening was Lawrence Welk with his "a-one and a-two" intros between folksy endorsements for Poligrip denture adhesive or Sominex sleeping tablets.

"Friends, do you ever have trouble falling asleep at night?"

Dad waited patiently through the song and dance acts for his favourite part of the show. The Champagne Music Makers would rise behind their music stands and play the big band dance tunes of the '30s and '40s. Dad would lean forward for the solos—clarinet, trumpet, saxophone—humming and bedool-ya-ing in his peculiar scat singing style.

When the champagne bubbles floated up behind the band, it meant the show was over. The Lawrence Welk musical family, swaying together, would sing:

Good night, sleep tight and pleasant dreams to you.
Here's a wish, and a prayer that every dream comes true...

Dad would go off to putter at his workbench, still humming. I would tune into reruns of *Felony Squad*, fantasizing about the young Dennis Cole, whose handsome face, blond hair and dark eyebrows provided the prototype for the man I planned to marry.

◊ ◊ ◊

BY MAY, the lawyers had worked out the financial details of our marriage separation. I began house hunting. My realtor was in her early fifties, divorced, with a graduate degree in business administration. I needed female wisdom (other than my mother's) for all phases of this move.

I wanted a character home with hardwood floors that would be big enough for my kids but small enough for me to manage. Mature trees and a mid-sized yard in a quiet, stable neighbourhood would be just right.

I was looking for Kingsland.

The realtor picked me up in her 4×4 truck. We talked about divorce and healing and *Women Who Run with the Wolves* as we travelled from property to property. We were Wild Women, breaking free of traditional roles and society's expectations. We were creative, independent and brave.

The first house had a nice yard but a dark, scary basement.

The second had hardwood floors but the bathroom needed repairs.

The third, a duplex, was new and modern but the yard was tiny and the street too busy.

Back in the truck, I fought back tears. This was all so hard. Looking for a house on my own. Taking care of it on my own. Being on my own.

Some wild woman.

The most courageous woman I'd ever known was my grandmother, Nan, who, during the Hungry Thirties, refused to go on Relief after her husband deserted the family.

"I went straight to the mayor of Saskatoon and demanded a job. Said I wouldn't leave his office until he gave me one. So he did."

Nan loved to tell this story over a drink of rye, ice clinking in the glass, cigarette smoke curling up around her face, blue eyes squinting.

There were other stories, too. During the war years, she became the first woman station agent for the Canadian National Railway, posted in Melville, Saskatchewan. She fought for her military widow's pension after her estranged husband died in 1953. She survived breast, throat and stomach cancer.

When she died at eighty-three, her funeral Mass was followed by a wake. Nan had always liked a good party. Friends and family sang together arm in arm, swaying and crying, and raised a glass to her memory: "God love 'er!"

I could use some of her courage right now.

On a sunny day in June, I found a small white house with green trim that was just right. I stepped into the front entryway and said, "I'll buy it."

There were hardwood floors (the Johnson paste wax kind) that led into a cozy living room with an east-facing window alcove and a built-in china cabinet. There were two bright bedrooms upstairs and a newly renovated bathroom with a pedestal sink. A narrow kitchen with tall white cupboards and a window that looked out onto a large wooden deck and backyard with an enormous poplar tree. The basement had been finished in panel board and carpet: a perfect rumpus room.

The house was furnished with antiques and flea market finds in various stages of refinishing; it felt inviting and calm. Its current owner was a woman, divorced, raising two teenage daughters on her own.

This had been her healing house, she told me. It would become mine.

The neighbourhood was called Mountview.

◇ ◇ ◇

WE MOVED IN that August. Across the street, my new neighbour jumped out of her truck and waved, her hair a tangle of auburn curls.

"Do you have kids?" she shouted, hauling grocery bags into her arms.

"Yeah. Two!"

"I have four! We'll have to get together. I'm Tracey."

I think I am going to love it here.

I arranged my faithful IKEA furniture, unpacked dishes, hung pictures and repotted plants. I hunted garage sales and the classified ads for missing pieces of home. Couch, kitchen table, bunk beds, barbeque.

My best garage sale find was a bright red gas lawnmower.

I could feel myself grinning ridiculously the first time I mowed my lawn, practising in the huge, forgiving backyard, and then—free of performance anxiety—roaring around to the front.

I began exploring new aisles in Canadian Tire, there among the men, looking for Roundup herbicide and eyeing the Kärcher power washers.

My dad loved the hardware department at Woolco. He would spend Saturday afternoons in what he called the "junketeria" sorting through bins of metal bits with his index finger, looking for just the right nut or bolt for his latest invention. These included an air conditioner for one of his import cars and a spiky metal microphone guard that kept Bill, overzealous singer for the Nova Tones, from getting too close to the mic.

Dad built inventions for us kids, too. Like a go-cart made from wood shelving, baby buggy wheels and a circular brass display rack pilfered from the garbage behind the local drugstore. You would sit on the thick, wooden running board and steer the brass rack while a good-natured friend pushed you up the street. Then you would coast back down, using your feet as brakes, stopping just short of the Cunninghams' driveway, where men in black T-shirts leaned in under the hood of a torn-apart Ford Galaxy.

In the spirit of this go-cart and his own Super Boy-Car from Eaton's, Dad had bought his grandsons a red Big Wheel Jeep. Its high-pitched whine and rhythmic *ka-thunk* over sidewalk cracks became, along with its towheaded drivers, a regular part of the Mountview landscape.

I decided—decreed—that my children would have a golden childhood like mine, despite the divorce. I had the setting, props and costumes (name brands only) ready. My cast of characters—maverick single mom and her two well-adjusted sons—would roll through a series of adventures that all worked out in the end. Failure was not in the script.

During the dog days of August, we walked to the outdoor pool on hot afternoons, towels rolled up under our arms. We went for picnics in the park and bike rides through shaded trails. I smiled at the words on the back of Robert's T-shirt as he pedalled ahead of me on the path: *No Fear*.

In September, our first-day-of-school picture tells the story. Robert is ready for grade two in new black high-tops, khaki shorts and crisp white shirt, his hair slicked down like Alfalfa's. Beside him is Michael, in red high-tops and shorts, clutching bear and blanket, happy to return to his heaven-sent dayhome mom, Sheila (who had taken gentle care of all of us during the upheaval of the past six months). I stand behind them wearing my serious navy blazer and white linen pants, ready for a new year of teaching junior high but determined to keep writing for magazines.

From my sunny front porch, I couldn't have foreseen the adventures of the year ahead. A couple weeks later, we woke up to an early snowfall. This wasn't particularly alarming until I looked out the kitchen window. The backyard was littered with poplar branches that had snapped under the weight of wet snow. When the snow had melted later that afternoon, I waded through the jagged boughs strewn across, impaling the ground. The boys were excited: building a tree fort had never been this easy. I was close to tears: I didn't know where to begin the clean-up.

"You can borrow my chainsaw," my next-door neighbour hollered over the fence, hoisting the machine and slinging the power cord across. "It's electric."

I had scarcely used a handsaw, much less a chainsaw. But I was knee-deep in branches and no one was coming to save me. I yanked the pull cord. The saw snarled to life, whining through slim poplar boughs, growling on the thicker ones. The noise brought the boys out of their fort. They stared in terror-filled amazement as their mother bucked those boughs into submission. I wished my own mother could have seen me.

In early October, Michael jumped from his top bunk, wearing his new Superman pajamas with the red cape, and smashed his elbow to smithereens. I was out of town at the time. Their dad was at a conference. Fortunately, our capable niece was babysitting and had called her parents for help. I arrived home to see a dejected Robert sitting alone on the curb. "I have no one to play with."

"Where's Michael? Did you two have a fight?"

My niece bolted out the front door. "Get back in your car. You need to go to the hospital."

My knees turned to water. I don't even remember the drive. As the nurse hurried me through hallways, I could hear Michael moaning. When he saw me, he started to wail in earnest. His dad was there within minutes. Together we bent over Michael, holding his hand, stroking his forehead, reassuring him as we waited, worrying, for the orthopedic specialist to arrive. It would be a long night of X-rays, consults and surgery that dawned on a rough day of post-op recovery. Three steel pins and a long thin scar (the first of many) would be the legacy of Superman's ill-fated flight.

Another new, less harrowing adventure began with Robert's first season playing Dynamite hockey, an apt description for the total shock this would be to my female upbringing. For me, skating meant freedom: twirling around on Kingsland's outdoor rink under night skies. I never much noticed what happened on the other side of those plywood boards apart from the harsh rasp of skate blades and the smack of pucks and sticks. The only thing familiar to me in this new hockey world was the damp fug of the dressing room. I'd never even considered all the gear. Shoulder pads, neck guards, elbow pads, shin guards, jock strap and cup were purchased and packed away in a Mighty Ducks hockey bag, but not until we'd had a dress rehearsal on the living room rug.

As Christmas approached with its stress-inducing imperatives, I was determined to hit all the marks. I shopped for clothes, books and toys—nearly braining myself with the last Top Corner Hockey game perched on the top shelf at Zellers. I strung outdoor lights on the front-yard junipers and mountain ash. I bought a Christmas tree, scrawny but real. The kids made gingerbread houses that collapsed under gumdrop roofs.

With the help of our mediator, we had parsed up the holiday schedule to give the kids equal time with both parents and grandparents. I would be alone on Christmas Eve. I planned to go to midnight Mass, since Robert was playing a shepherd in the Christmas pageant. The church was predictably packed so I had to sit on the sharp brick ledge that covered the radiator at the back of the church. I could see my former family—husband, mother- and father-in-law, sisters- and brothers-in-law, nieces—sitting with my two sons in a pew near the front. Michael turned around and saw me. He waved wildly, entreating me to come join the family. When I didn't move, he ran up the aisle to the back of the church and sat beside me, on the humble bricks, for the rest of the service.

It would be a year of adjustment for all of us. Michael began playschool a couple days a week, but refused to go on any of their field trips. He didn't want to go anywhere beyond the safe, familiar zones of our houses and his dayhome and the basement of Sunnyside playschool. He didn't stay in his own bed most nights, crawling in to sleep beside me instead, where he muttered and kicked at imaginary foes.

"I wish I had magic powers," Michael told me one night before he drifted off.

I asked him why, expecting the usual answers. Superhero powers, birthdays every day.

"I'd make you and Dad married again," he said.

I couldn't breathe at first. Then I rushed in with really good reasons. We hadn't been happy together. We didn't get along. Didn't he remember the arguments?

"That would be part of my magic. You wouldn't fight anymore."

At swimming lessons in April, Robert, almost eight, refused to go into the water, no matter how much I coaxed or admonished. He sat on the pool edge, arms crossed, shivering in fluorescent-green shorts. This was strange; he hadn't done this since he was three.

"Maybe it's because you're getting a divorce," said the teenage swimming instructor, who somehow knew our story. I could have kicked her brash butt into the deep end.

I railed against this single-parent stigma that insinuated its way into parent-teacher interviews, church events, hockey meetings, casual conversations. There was an assumption that any problems my kids might have—now and forever—would be a direct result of the separation, the divorce, the "broken home." I was determined that we—the kids, their dad and me—would come through it stronger, more resilient, maybe even happier.

A few days after the pool incident, I sat beside Robert at the kitchen table, where he was doing his homework. Quiet and circumspect, he'd always kept his feelings to himself.

"We've been through a lot of changes this year," I say.

"Yeah." He concentrates on his drawing. He's a talented artist.

"Some things have been hard but some good things have happened, too. Right?"

He doesn't look up. "I don't want to talk about this."

A few days later, I gave him a blank sketchbook. "Just in case you want to draw about it."

In late May, big plans were afoot for the annual family dance at the school. I had planned not to go, but the boys insisted. They loved racing around the darkened gym pulsing with laser lights and Aqua songs. I sat on the bleachers, sipping orange drink from McDonald's, watching adults mingle and kids dart by. I suddenly realized how many single parents were there—separated, divorced, never-married-in-the-first-place—enjoying the dance as a family. For me, it was a moment of grace.

That first year, my sons and I triumphed over windstorms, snowstorms and basement floods. We'd fixed broken windows, mended broken bones and patched up our hearts.

So this is happiness, I said to myself, sitting alone on my back deck one warm night in June. Staring at the full moon, listening to distant wind chimes, learning to live with some suspense.

{ NINE }

SUNDAY AFTERNOON. SUPERSTORE. I'm stocking up for the busy week ahead.

A display of Pyrex glassware is stacked in the centre aisle a few feet away. A pie plate slips from the pile, slides down toward the floor and shatters. A second plate follows, lemming-like, down to the same fate.

I wanted to grab the third plate, but froze. What if everyone thinks I caused this? What if they blame me for the whole mess? What if they make me pay for it?

I turn away, feigning a sudden interest in Tie 'n Toss garbage bags, appearing startled by the smash of glass behind me. I glance over my shoulder at the heap of shards.

I could have saved the Pyrex.

Above me, a giant photo board of a smiling family—two parents, two kids—hangs suspended in a metal-girded sky.

I could have saved my family.

I stand exposed in the fluorescent glare.

A tingle snakes across my neck. A hot flush creeps from scalp to forehead. I take an extra big breath. And another. Am I hyperventilating? There's a package of brown lunch bags on the shelf in front of me. I could rip one open, bunch it up, breathe into it slowly. Normally.

Don't be crazy.

I rush out of the store and drive the twenty blocks home to Mountview.

Sanctuary.

My house wraps me inside its protective walls. I can breathe again.

I try to dismiss the entire incident as a result of too much caffeine. Not enough exercise. Maybe a rogue wave of anxiety caused by cavernous big-box stores. Or is it guilt?

A few weeks later, I'm driving north from Calgary just at the point where the Deerfoot Trail narrows and becomes Highway 2. Where the frenzy of merge and pass decreases and you notice prairie and sky and can breathe a little easier.

Suddenly, I can't find the bottom of my lungs. My breath comes in quick, shallow scoops. Prickles of heat race across my scalp, forehead and cheeks. I feel shivers up my spine.

It's happening again.

What should I do?

I know someone in Airdrie. I could stop in for coffee and a perfectly normal chat. Or I could take the next exit south, back to my parents'.

And say what? That I'm too scared to drive to my own house?

I have a sudden image of my mother clambering into my car, offering to keep me company. The driving equivalent of her sitting on my bed, yawning, until I fall asleep.

I can't figure out what's worse. Driving in fear or admitting this new fear to my parents, unleashing the "we told you so" chorus I suspect is lying dormant not only in them but in those Hummel figurines on their coffee table and Vermeer's milkmaid on the wall: *If you'd never left your marriage, if you'd never left the Kingdom, you would never know this fear.*

I look at my kids in the rear-view mirror, staring calmly out the window, oblivious to my front-seat drama.

I try to breathe deeply.

My heart beats staccato against my chest. Is this a heart attack?

I reach for a cassette tape. Summon Sharon, Lois and Bram from the glove compartment.

I am slowly going crazy. One two three four five six switch. Crazy going slowly am I . . .

I go to see my doctor. I'm feeling strange, I tell her. Every time I drive further than the city limits, I get these weird sensations. Kind of breathless. Sort of dizzy. A little scared. Like I might lose control.

(Am I losing control?)

The doctor asks about my work, the kids, the marriage that she knows is over. I'd always sensed she hoped for reconciliation. Maybe she thinks this is a sign that I should go back to where I belong.

She prescribes a relaxant—something to get me over this hump. It's very mild, she assures me. I take the prescription, scrawled with symbols and "No repeats." Slowly, I walk downstairs to the clinic pharmacy.

I'm the only customer in the store. The pharmacist greets me in a familiar way. He's filled my prescriptions before. He reaches down from his platform to hand me the package, hesitates, then gently touches my shoulder.

"You need to smile more."

He never says that when he gives me penicillin. I am instantly suspicious of these tiny green pills. I read: "Long-term or excessive use of this medication can cause dependency." Now I'm scared. *Use caution while driving...* I start to laugh. So much for reducing my anxiety on the road.

I flush the Ativan down the toilet.

I buy an suv instead.

A Jeep Cherokee that could four-wheel-drive through snow and mud and over my interior terrain of fear. It is red. The colour of courage.

◊ ◊ ◊

MY DAD TAUGHT ME to drive when I was fifteen. On Sunday afternoons in a deserted Chinook Centre parking lot, he would explain the mysteries of the standard-shift transmission and his time-tested method of pre-selecting the gears. "Always know what gear you'll need next."

Dad taught all of us to drive, beginning with my mother, who learned in bumpy fields on the edge of Kingsland while we three girls bounced along in the back seat. Sometimes, we bailed out and tied strings over gopher holes, the white Epic lurching around us.

Mom practised hill starts on the steep, lonely road by the Elephant Brand Fertilizer plant. As we gently coasted backwards, she jammed the stickshift, searching for first gear, her knuckles a white claw. I prayed to the St. Christopher magnet on the dashboard. The clutch grabbed, mercifully, inching us uphill.

Mom had all her routes worked out in advance, with minimal hills and few left turns. Driving downtown with her was frightening, particularly the 4th Street underpass by Eaton's. She never drove much outside the city limits.

For me, highway driving became a symbolic act of courage, imagining my journey traced out in a dotted line on a map, like in the old movies. Calgary to Edmonton. Calgary to Radium. Calgary to Vernon. I didn't go far, odometrically speaking, but I still remember that feeling of power on the summit of Rogers Pass, flags waving, mountains witnessing. I was brave and absolutely on my own.

I never did much of the highway driving after I got married, deferring to some old notion that men drive the long distances. I fretted about traffic, road and weather conditions from the passenger seat instead, where I doled out snacks and drinks for the kids, and felt my world begin to shrink.

It is a sunny, blue-sky winter day. Highway 2, clear and dry, stretches straight ahead.

A lovely day for a drive, my mother would say.

A perfect day for the crucible.

I shift my new Jeep into fifth gear, determined to enjoy this. Like I used to.

Alone.

Alone.

I shake off a tremor of uneasiness, take a deep breath.

Was that a complete breath?

I reach for another, hyperaware.

Are you breathing properly?

I turn on the radio. Sing.

My mouth is desert-dry. I can hardly swallow.

What if you choke?

I look at the scenery. The prairie landscape through the windshield is unfamiliar, surreal. My head feels dizzy, swirling.

What if you pass out? What if you crash?

I scan the highway for a reassuring green sign. Twenty kilometres to the next town. There's a gas station by the overpass. I can pull in there if I have to.

And what? Panic completely? Sob hysterically? Run shrieking onto the highway?

I'm afraid to keep driving.

I'm more afraid to stop.

⌂ ⌂ ⌂

THE ANXIETY GROWS. Shape-shifts. Not only on highway drives but on solitary walks and bike rides. Or on the quick flights to Vancouver that I used to love. Whenever I am out on my own, wisps of worry gather into clouds that hide the sun. Ubiquitous anxiety.

I scare myself with stories heard in casual conversation. A teacher who fell apart in her classroom. A mother who ran screaming out of her house onto the street. A widow with agoraphobia so severe she had to be moved to her new house across town in a holiday trailer.

The Nervous Breakdown.

I still picture it as I did in childhood. A woman—always a woman—in a floral housedress and Phentex knit slippers lies curled up on the kitchen floor shaking uncontrollably.

Going Off the Deep End.

I see myself at nine, dripping wet, shivering, toes curled around the tile edge of the YMCA swimming pool. I stare into deep blue fear that smells of chlorine.

Cracking Up.

Pyrex plates slipping, sliding and crashing to the floor.

Do I need to go see my psychologist?

It's been two years since my last session. I've left a marriage, bought a house, shifted careers, raised kids. If there were Brownie badges for critical life events, I could fill up an entire sleeve. Could this anxiety be a reaction to all of that, some post-traumatic stress that I haven't admitted?

Maybe mental health requires regularly scheduled maintenance, like a car.

Problem is, I don't feel sad. Or depressed. Most days, I like my life. So why the anxiousness, these almost-but-not-quite panic attacks?

Panic. A word derived from Pan, the mythic god of lonely, wild places who scared travellers with eerie sounds and hair-raising sensations. He was frightening to look at, too, with the head and torso of a man, legs and horns of a goat. Just like the devil in the middle-drawer *Children's Illustrated Bible*.

Is that what this panic could be? Am I being punished for all my sins?

In my good-manners-in-God's-house phase, Confession would have been the surefire, silver-bullet solution. Not now. There is not enough space behind that confessional door, the red light glowing crossly above, for the story behind the sins.

Forgive me, Father, for I have sinned.

It has been fifteen years since my last Confession.

These are my sins:

Number One: I am a bad Catholic.

Honestly? Here's my story.

I've been avoiding church because the God who lives there had such high hopes and is very disappointed. I'm afraid to sit in the wooden pew surrounded by close-knit, can-do, nuclear families. The undivorced, unbroken Morally Superiors.

(In my soul's defence, I did seek a fresh spiritual experience one Sunday at the Sunnyside United Church. People chatted across the pews. Children clambered over and under. If my mother had been there, they would have been frozen on the spot by her icy glares. This was much too casual. Not enough holy icons or stained glass. No sickly sweet incense or Sanctus bells. The pastor was too young and—is that his pregnant wife in the front pew?—too virile. What was this bread with grape juice ritual and why was there a four-year-old in the Communion line ahead of me?)

Going to church feels like going to my parents' house. I will always be a child, flustered by adult responsibilities, incapable of making good decisions.

Which brings me to Sin Number Two: I am a bad daughter.

My dad remains perplexed—no, insulted—by my choices. He points out that he and Mom have beat the odds: fifty percent of marriages in North America end in divorce. Actuarially speaking, their marriage has been a stellar success.

Mom is hurt by my silence and distance after years of knowing everything about me. She leans close to me, proffers her lips for the compulsory kiss hello. She touches my hair ("New highlights?"), strokes my sleeve ("New sweater?"), in search of the old intimacy. I back away from her, arms folded across my chest.

Their immaculate house with the well-stocked fridge and cupboards is poised for family gatherings of three daughters and four grandsons, so far. Sons-in-law are a work-in-progress. My wedding picture still hangs above their fireplace. Bride and groom, best man, matron of honour and two sets of parents all arranged on a Persian carpet.

Is that nostalgia or sabotage?

I tell my mom that she can take that picture down any-time. The marriage is officially over. This is my house, she says, snarky as a teenager, I can leave the picture there if I want. Thanks for validating the last two years of my life, I tell her. I hang the picture upside down in passive Gandhi-like resistance, a nicely symbolic statement of how my life has shifted direction. She offers to drape a black cloth over it. Why not hang up your own wedding picture, I ask, the one you've kept stashed in a drawer for the past forty years?

Sparks of resentment fly between us. We've never clashed like this before. Now, I put on my armour and stand my ground. During our last visit, Robert felt sick late one night and called out for me. Mom clambered out of her bed to help me help Robert throw up. "Get the hell away from me," I'd hissed. "I can take care of my own kid!"

Sin Number Three: I am a bad mother.

At least according to that glossy Mother's Day ad for pricey perfume from Eaton's. It reminds every consumer-of-woman-born about those qualities we need to thank mothers for, each word in sweet pastel hues:

Patience. Affection. Understanding.

I admit it. Single-parenting is tougher than I thought. Those early morning hockey games where the only thanks I get is a snarl that I tie skates too loose. Those theme birthday parties and relentless treat bags. Batman. Space Jam. Canned Spam. Those Christmas Eve shopping and wrapping frenzies where, haunted by the ghost of perfect Christmases past, I overspend, undersleep and want to throw rock-hard shortbread at my spoiled children every blessed Christmas morning.

Security. Support. Trust.

I worry about money. A lot. The rising costs of the kids and their activities makes me feel guilty about my decision to write more and teach less.

I confess. There's too much fast food and not enough home-cooked dinners. Too much Nintendo and not enough Yahtzee. Too much preoccupied parent and not enough back-yard soccer.

On the golden childhood standard, I am more often wicked stepmother than fairy godmother, prone to tantrums and repeating "I hate this" like a mantra.

The kids, eyes downcast, wait for the storm to pass.

Guidance. Encouragement. Inspiration.

I *did* take the kids to the symphony performance of *Beethoven Lives Upstairs*. This would provide musical enrichment, I reasoned, since I'd dropped the ball on the kids' piano lessons, an unwieldy blend of portable keyboards, Popsicle stick puppets and parent participation.

(Piano lessons were simpler when I was a kid. All my mom had to do was set the timer on the stove or—on the odd occasion when I kicked the piano with a reverberating, satisfying thud—spank me and send me to my room.)

We get ready for the concert. Robert's dress pants end just above his ankles. The button pops on the waistband. What's wrong with jeans? he'd like to know. Michael's runners have no laces; the tongues splay in sloppy defiance. We arrive late. The boys slump down in their seats in the audience, shaggy hair just sprung from reluctantly removed ball caps. I poke them to sit up straight and hiss at them to keep quiet. They cheer loudly when the performance ends. That was so boring, they agree. Beside me, a husband and wife applaud politely with their three well-mannered, impeccably dressed sons with an appreciation for Beethoven.

I hate this. I hate this. I hate this.

These are my sins.

May God the Father forgive me and make me true to His spirit.

It's no use. I'm stuck in the old rules of Confession. In order for these sins to be forgiven, I have to admit that everything I'm doing is wrong.

But *that* feels like a lie.

◊ ◊ ◊

INSOMNIA MOVES BACK IN, dragging every piece of dread-filled baggage from twenty years before. I had almost forgotten about those months of wide-awake exhaustion. They'd become a blip in my memory, a tale for Ripley's Believe It or Not!, like someone who'd had the hiccups for a year.

I consider my options.

I think about calling my sister Kim. She helped with this issue before. But her new husband might answer. Sleepy. Surly. Sighing through the phone line with male derision.

At times, women have uncontrollable emotions.

Call my mom? Just pick up the phone and admit it. I need to come home to sleep. And crack up.

Somewhere inside me, a gentle voice reassures.

You know you're not crazy.

I get up, snap on the light, grab my pen.

If I can't sleep, I might as well use the time productively.

The night shift begins.

I write on yellow newsprint about things I don't want to write about.

"I am a woman who is afraid to be alone."

I hate writing this personal shit.

Write.

This is not the kind of writing that counts. I should be writing magazine articles like "Six Survival Skills for Stressed Single Parents" or "Risky Business: Why Rebound Relationships Fail."

Write.

"I am a forty-year-old woman who is afraid to be alone."

This is stupid-fucking-useless-navel-gazing.

Write.

"I feel fear rise in tingling palms and dizzy head as I drive alone on highways in a red Jeep I bought to keep me safe. What if I get lost? What if no one knows where I am? Like Hansel and Gretel trying to find their way home, I look for bread crumbs along the highways I drive. Familiar green road signs, full-service gas stations, grounding conversations on cellular phones…"

I write how I have always been afraid.

Afraid of nighttime in my bedroom. Afraid of being the last one to fall asleep. Afraid of the dark behind heavy closet doors that roll like thunder. Afraid of my Nancy Drew books with their yellow spines and scary covers.

Nancy Drew was not afraid of anything.

Suddenly, mysteriously, I feel myself smiling.

◊ ◊ ◊

SHE FLICKS ON *her signal light, downshifts and pulls into the gas station parking lot.*

She takes a couple deep breaths, leans her head back, squeezes her eyes against hot, frustrated tears.

It's happening again. The anxiousness—the could-be-panic (-but-you-never-know-for-sure).

She hears a knock on the side window, opens her eyes. An attractive young woman is standing beside her Jeep. Flustered, she rolls down the window.

"Excuse me, ma'am," the young woman says, "I saw that you pulled over rather suddenly. Do you require some assistance?"

No, the woman replies, mumbling something about needing a bathroom break.

"Are you certain, ma'am? I have some smelling salts here in my handbag."

No, the older woman insists that she is fine. Just needs to stretch her legs. Quit calling me ma'am, she'd like to add.

The young woman is relentlessly helpful.

"An egg salad sandwich, perhaps? I was just setting out for a picnic in my blue convertible roadster. I have plenty of sandwiches. My housekeeper made them for me."

Something about this young woman is familiar. She is dressed in a fetching pink sheath dress with matching pumps. Slim and attractive, she has blue eyes and blondish-brownish-reddish hair one might almost call—titian.

"*You're Nancy Drew!*"

The older woman is suddenly aware of her rumpled grey sweatsuit, minimal makeup and hair colour nowhere near titian. She glances furtively around the parking lot.

"Is someone pursuing you?" Nancy queries. "A stranger or a kidnapper? A sinister man with a beard?"

"No, no. Nothing like that," she responds sheepishly. "I pulled over because I feel this weird anxiety every time I find myself alone—especially when I'm driving on the highway. It's a mystery to me," she adds wanly.

"Oh, I can't resist a good mystery." Nancy smiles, her blue eyes sparkling. "I've been wondering when my next mystery would come along. My first was the Secret of the Old Clock and I recently solved The Clue in the—"

"Nancy," the woman interrupts, "I don't think all my silly fears would make a very good mystery. I used to be afraid of most of the scenes on the covers of your books. Especially The Ghost of Blackwood Hall. You were peering around the doorway with your flashlight. Brave as ever. Maybe that's because your chums were on the cover with you—the trim, boyish George Fayne and the pretty but slightly plump Bess Marvin. Anyway, as far as your next great mystery goes, I haven't got many clues for you to go on."

Nancy laughs. "Most of the people in River Heights who ask me for help have no clue either."

The older woman smiles slightly, hesitates. "Why do I feel so anxious when I'm on my own? Am I going crazy?"

"I've never solved a psychological mystery," admits Nancy. "Just the everyday mysteries around River Heights. Jewel thieves, counterfeiters, pickpockets, flim-flammers. Sometimes my *sleuthing takes me to Scotland, New Orleans or Egypt, hot on the trail of a mystery."*

"I've often wondered how you can afford all those trips," the older woman jests. "Seriously, Nancy, I can hardly travel around Alberta these days. I feel uneasy and I want to know why. Can you help me?"

"Is there some horribly traumatic event in your past?" Nancy queries. "Have you, for instance, ever stepped into a quagmire? Been abducted on a mini-submarine? Been chloroformed by racketeers posing as mediums?"

"No, no. Nothing like that. I had a normal childhood. Very stable."

The young sleuth does not respond, but her eyes dart instinctively around the older woman's Jeep, looking for additional clues. To-go cups and fast-food wrappers suggest untidy children with poor nutritional habits.

"Is your father a distinguished criminal lawyer?" Nancy asks.

"No, he sold electric heating cables."

"My father is Carson Drew. He often enlists my help with his puzzling cases."

"You two seem very close," the older woman says wistfully.

Maybe it is fathers who make us brave after all.

{ TEN }

THE FOOTHILLS HOSPITAL in Calgary sits on the crest of a northwest hill, overlooking the Bow River and the traffic of 16th Avenue. Whenever anyone in our family has had to stay at the Foothills, it is serious business: high-risk pregnancy, retina repair, heart surgery.

My father has just had a quadruple bypass. He is seventy-nine.

My sister Kim and I travel to the hospital over the Glenmore Causeway to Crowchild Trail, cross the bridge onto Memorial Drive and climb steep hills through neighbourhoods that used to be on the edge of the city. Going north in Calgary has always made me nervous—away from our safe southwest quadrant.

Maybe it began with that yearly test of bravery: the Kiwanis Music Festival. I would rehearse Bach's *Minuet in G* on my lap as we travelled the length of 14th Street to the Jubilee Auditorium, the hilltop monolith of marble and brick with the statue of Robert the Bruce in front, impervious to my anxiety.

Foothills hospital is bigger than I remember and the parking lot sign says "Full." The attendant waves us through anyway. Near the entrance, a cluster of patients shiver, clutching their hospital housecoats tightly, as they smoke beside their IV poles. It is a warm day for February. The automatic doors squeak open as we enter. I feel that familiar guilt about how fortunate I am to be able to walk into the hospital and not have to stay indefinitely.

You could be in a wheelchair.

The lobby is large and loud. There is a Good Earth Café nearby, offering scones with white chocolate and raspberries and gourmet coffee served at bistro tables—enough to make you feel like you're in the food court of a mall instead of a hospital. Temporarily.

No time for coffee now. My sister and I move through the crowd at the elevators. We push the arrow and wait. I read the benefactors' names engraved on the marble walls. The elevator rings. Doors open and shut. My stomach lurches—part elevator, part fear. I don't know what to expect.

I had last seen Dad two weeks earlier. He'd been admitted to the Rockyview hospital for routine tests. He'd had trouble sleeping for several nights in a row. Shortness of breath. Racing heart. Cold sweats. Was this just anxiety or something more? The doctors wanted to be sure.

Stress tests were scheduled for later that week at the Foothills hospital.

Within hours of those tests, everything changed. The heart specialist scheduled bypass surgery for the next morning, Saturday. While the doctors operated, I watched my seven-year-old play hockey in an arena far away. Michael, in his bright red helmet, skated end to end. That's what the coaches liked to see: heart and hustle.

My sister called me on my cell phone. "You should come to Calgary now."

On the Cardiac Intensive Care Unit at the Foothills, we wait in a small room with green vinyl couches and chairs of grey moulded plastic. A window faces north, overlooking the big yellow *H* of the helicopter landing pad. *H* is for heart. Kim picks up the phone and asks permission to enter the ward. She is so calm and controlled. She rarely cries. Of all of us, she is still the closest to Dad.

We walk through heavy double doors into a long room with a row of beds, each occupied by a person silent and still. They look like they are napping, no struggle here at all. Mom is sitting beside the bed. She jumps up when we arrive—relieved to assume her mother role.

I don't recognize my father. He looks dead—or how I imagine dead would look. Hair brushed smoothly back from his forehead, waxen and grey. I am afraid to touch him; I don't know how.

I make myself reach for his hand. It is cold.

"We have to lower the body temperature during surgery," the nurse explains, repositioning bags filled with blood and urine hanging beneath the bed.

"I think I'm going to be sick."

Mom is instantly at my side. Solicitous. Ridiculous. I'm not the one who is dying here.

The nurse sits me in a chair, gives me a glass of water and resumes her post in front of a computer screen that monitors all things chemical and electrical keeping my father alive.

I suddenly remember all those summer holiday side trips to hydroelectric dams: Duncan, Portage Mountain, Mica Creek. Concrete shrines to progress, science and technology: Dad's religion.

"You can see how water generates electricity," Dad would tell us, driving into empty parking lots, scouting for information booths.

I would stare at the water spillways, terrified. Spellbound by their rush and force and spray.

Why have I always been afraid?

Afraid of the transformer towers that flank the freeways. Criss-crosses of steel and metal coils strung with black-wire skipping ropes that buzz. (They will electrocute you if you get too close.)

I was afraid when the trolley cables jumped the track on the old green-and-white city buses. Sparks crackle. Lights flicker. The bus driver leaps out and pulls on the wires behind the back window. The motor hums back to life.

I stare at Dad in his hospital bed, white sheets tucked up to his chin.

Is there some father–daughter connection we have missed? If I lie down now on the bed beside him, patch into his electrical circuits, will it galvanize something in me that feels like calm?

△ △ △

LATER THAT NIGHT, back at the house in Kingsland, I pull all the photo albums out of the bottom drawer of Dad's dresser. I look through the black-and-white photos of our childhood, the dates abbreviated on scalloped edges. There are so few pictures of Dad, relegated to infrastructure. There could be no heart-to-hearts.

DEC '63

Here's Mom and us three little girls in front of the Christmas tree. We are dressed in new white smock tops with hand-embroidered treble clefs on each. Mom is wearing a smart tartan dress and her hair is nicely curled. I hold my new doll by the arm and frown at the photographer, who must be Dad, staring down into the Kodak Brownie camera and telling us to smile. We hear the pop of the flashbulb and smell burning glass. We blink white spots afterward.

There's my favourite Christmas ornament hanging on the tree—a small gold saxophone.

FEB '64

This is a picture of Dad. Two, actually. A haunting double exposure. In the clearer picture Dad sits in the rocking chair and smiles at Robin and me, decked out in our new Christmas pajamas, toques and mitts beside a candy-striped doll stroller.

Over this picture is another, transparent and ghostly. Dad sits alone in his downstairs office, looking straight at the camera, playing his saxophone. He looks like he is rising out of our heads.

AUG '65

I remember this day in Jasper. I am sitting alone on the riverbank, one knee pulled up to my chest, unaware of any camera. I have been told to tie my own saddle shoes (grade one would be starting soon) and to hurry up. My sisters are nowhere in sight. I remember the panic that gripped me there on the rocks. Sock-footed with my shoelaces in knots, I was going to be left alone with the bears.

Whoever took this photo intended it for the grown-up I would become. It might have been my mother—before she realized that growing up meant growing apart. Or maybe it was Dad, teaching me to rely on myself.

△ △ △

DAD DIED THAT NIGHT.

Briefly.

Three hundred kilojoules of electricity brought him back to life, zapping every last bit of his own will to live.

On the day Dad came home from the hospital, the ceiling tiles in his downstairs office fell in a single, giant whoosh to the floor. Dad sat upstairs in the living room staring straight ahead, oxygen tank clicking rhythmically beside him, as if he knew his world had collapsed beneath him.

A world of saxophone swing tunes, newspaper clippings, oddball inventions and quirky how-to's. One yellow square set whimsically at its centre.

Dad has given me enough.

◌ ◌ ◌

CRISIS PASSED, we return to our regular lives. My mother waves goodbye to me from the front porch. She looks so small and frail, hunched over with this new burden of my father's convalescence.

I don't go home right away, feeling a familiar tremor of anxiety for the highway drive ahead. I stop in at Chinook Centre, now a sprawling megamall with ancient Egyptian scarabs on one end and space-age spires on the other.

Woodward's is long gone. I see some older ladies shopping, all dressed up with their hair in beauty parlour sets, wistful for afternoon coffee in the Macleod Room. They wander through the aisles and ride the escalators, remembering, like some phantom limb after an amputation, how this place used to feel.

I search for traces of the old Chinook. I find the green terrazzo stairs that lead to the lower mall. Slide my hand down the same silver railing. No more shoe repair or barber shop. No more library. Only the bowling alley rumbles on from its 1960s time warp.

They say that the shopping malls of the late twentieth-century have become our cathedrals. Huge places for people to gather and share the ritual of retail. I feel calm here—much calmer than I do in church—as I gather up my memories. The quiet wonder of the library, the gentle excitement of Christmas, the simple joy of swivelling side to side on the lunch-counter stools in Kresge's, watching grape juice splash inside glass JetStream coolers.

I wander into the new big bookstore. Browsing through the self-help section, I act casual and noncommittal—like I'm only killing time until the coffee barista bellows "Moc-cachino vente!" across the aisles.

There are several books about anxiety, panic and pho-bias on the shelf. Even Dale Carnegie, the founding father of self-help, lives on in *How to Stop Worrying and Start Living*.

I pick up a more current publication written by a psy-chologist with a stern, serious name followed by "PhD." The book is big, bulky and distressingly obvious. I flip through the pages. Feign disinterest.

Of all the anxiety disorders, agoraphobia is the most preva-lent. It is estimated that one in twenty, or about five percent of the general population, suffers from varying degrees of agora-phobia ... The word agoraphobia *means fear of open spaces.*

Nope. Not me. Not afraid of that.

However, the essence of agoraphobia is a fear of panic attacks. If you suffer from agoraphobia, you are afraid of being in situations from which escape might be difficult—or in which help might be unavailable—if you suddenly had a panic attack. You may avoid grocery stores...

Superstore!

Perhaps the most common feature of agoraphobia is anxiety about being far away from home or far from a "safe person" (usually your spouse, partner, a parent, or anyone to whom you have a primary attachment).

That's me! Weaving a safety net of family and friends. Even my two sons seem more reliable than me.

You may completely avoid driving alone or may be afraid of driving alone beyond a certain short distance from home.

I feel my face flush with embarrassment. How could he know this about me? Has Nancy Drew been Morse-coding him from the young reader shelves?

I stand in the checkout line, the book clutched tight against my chest. I avoid eye contact with the cashier in my rush to get out of the store. To appear normal.

Wait. I have always been afraid to be alone, but I am not alone in my fear. Maybe this book will help me.

Later, while leaving the parkade labyrinth beneath Chinook Centre, I spot the square exterior tiles of Woodward's, once jade green, now painted stark white.

Chinook Centre may have reinvented itself, but its solid foundation remains. Brick and cement, but magic just the same.

ELEVEN

THERE WAS a new man in my life.

He brought companionship, adventure and a breathless kind of hope. I called him my Swiss Guide.

This nickname came from a museum exhibit we'd seen about the history of the Swiss guides in Canada. They were hired in 1899 by the Canadian Pacific Railway to lead wealthy tourists up the treacherous mountains around Banff and Lake Louise. Black-and-white photos showed men in three-piece suits and women in shirtwaists and long skirts sitting on glaciers, drinking tea from china cups.

There was an unforgettable photograph of a woman climber, in functional (yet stylish) woolen knickers, standing knee-deep in snow on a steep slope. She looked confident and secure, roped onto her rugged, capable Swiss guide in plaid shirt and broad-brimmed hat.

I felt happy and secure with my guide, too. We hiked and cycled and canoed into places I'd never been. He loved the outdoors and had travelled the world. Whenever I was with him, I felt safe, less anxious. This was good. I wanted to be fun and low-maintenance in this new relationship.

We plan a weekend getaway to the mountains. Clear blue sky and crisp autumn air hint of the snow to come. A perfect morning for strolling down the main street with a gourmet coffee. We wander past a store called Slick Rock—a name appropriated from some place in Utah for the extreme out-door adventure crowd of western Canada.

"Going Out of Business!" says a sign in the window. "Everything Must Go!"

What luck! A sale of high-end clothing and footwear.

Inside, I hear the salesman chat with a customer at the cash desk. She is buying a black Woolrich turtleneck. How extreme.

"Where are you from?" he asks her.

"Winnipeg."

He smiles warmly. "All women from Winnipeg are beautiful."

Slick talk.

I interrupt, politely, to ask the price of a bulky-knit Peru-vian sweater. I can picture myself wearing it while walking along some woodland path in spring.

"That's a *sale* price?" I ask, momentarily stunned.

He glares at me icily.

"Yes. That's the *sale* price."

He blows a short exasperated breath through his teeth and shakes his head.

"Shit," he mutters.

I feel my face flame with shame. Not only am I a cheapskate, I'm not from Winnipeg. I'm not beautiful. I'm a horrible person rushing into a rebound relationship.

Of course I deserve his contempt.

△ △ △

I ADMIT IT. I was trying to build this new relationship slowly, but my hopes raced wildly ahead. We talked late into the night about where we might travel. We took long drives in the country to look at acreages (his dream) with room to write (mine). We spoke about blending our families with a *Yours, Mine and Ours* happy ending.

I'd been living on my own for a while. I didn't want to live on my own forever. I envied other families I saw on camping trips sharing all those adventures: biking, boating, campfires, ghost stories after dark. I wanted that family feeling again. I wanted a man back in the picture. Not only for companionship but to set up the tent and build the fire.

Conflicts began erupting on fault lines that were eerily familiar. My emotional discourses. His stony silences. I wanted commitment; he wanted time. Time to work out his feelings about leaving his own marriage. Time to figure out a way to see more of his young son.

As he hesitated, my anxiety escalated. I avoided doing the usual things that brought the anxious feelings in. Highway driving, solitary walks. My avoidance only made things worse. Soon I was uneasy shopping at the corner grocery store or in the aisles between the tall shelves of Canadian Tire. Even at my sons' soccer games, I'd feel spacey, detached, as I watched them dart around the field, a bright-coloured blur. When I began to feel edgy in my beloved Mountview home, I knew my world was shrinking. Again.

I hated this helpless part of myself. I worked hard to hide it from him. Admitting it only on pages of yellow newsprint.

I am a woman who is afraid to be alone.

We were on a bike ride in the mountains that spring. My Swiss Guide was ahead of me on the trail, then suddenly out of sight around a bend. I sped up to catch him. Chest heaving, heart pounding, I rounded the curve. He was gone. The deserted path branched into two. Which way did he go? I shouted his name. No answer. Shouted again, Louder. I could hear the panic rise in my voice. I was afraid to keep going; I was more afraid to stop. I kept to the wider path, pedalling hard, shouting, gasping, praying to see him before I...what? Collapsed? Exploded? Endless minutes later, I spotted his plaid shirt through the trees. Relief poured through me. He was stopped on the path, straddling his bike, reading the trail map. I flew at him like a banshee, my tires spitting gravel, brakes squealing.

"Why didn't you answer me? Why didn't you look back? Why didn't you wait?"

He thought I knew the way. He thought I could keep up. He wondered why I was freaking out.

I threw down my bike, stomped off the trail and sat, fuming, on the grass. I wrapped my arms around my knees and dropped my head down.

Until the shame rose up.

I had to tell him. So I did, sort of.

"Sometimes I get these scary feelings when I am all alone. Especially in a forest."

He was kind, concerned and completely mystified. (What are you afraid of, bears?)

He hunkered down on the ground beside me, put his arm around my shoulders and told me he would always take care of me.

We looked at acreages on our drive back to the city, building castles in the sky.

The bike path incident showed me one uncomfortable truth.

That little girl inside me was *still* not quite sure the adult could handle things. Sending up distress signals through ragged breath and racing heart. We can't do this! Get help! Find a grown-up!

It was that albatross thing again. Still afraid to be all, all alone.

I knew I was pushing too hard to make this relationship permanent. The foundation was strong, I assured myself. We'd both been married before. We'd been on our own as single parents. This wasn't our first castle.

And then I remembered Kenilworth.

This was a real castle I'd seen on a trip to England years ago. It was summer but the day was cold and damp. Through the windows of the tour bus, the spires of Kenilworth rose in the mist. Reddish stone against dark green hedgerows. The castle was a ruin, missing its top half. Our tour guide explained that Kenilworth had been used as an upside-down quarry. Its walls had been broken apart, its stones carried off and used as foundation for other strongholds and castles nearby.

I kept thinking of that ruined castle as I rushed into building another.

There could be no new castle until I found this new cornerstone: the courage to be on my own.

No Prince Charming or Swiss Guide needed to save me.

We broke up.

He bought his acreage to build his dream home. I stayed in my Mountview bungalow to write.

I knew this was the right thing to do.

"We need to take a break," I'd told him. I'd sounded so rational and mature.

Truth is, every morning since our spring breakup, I wake up and immediately start to cry. Uncontrollable, irrational, blubbering like a baby.

Truth is, I'm devastated.

I buy a blue coil-bound notebook. I call it my "Deconstruction Journal," where I let myself write all manner of truly personal shit.

I hear you are working on your own castle now. I hope it fucks up and gets really expensive. You told me you wanted to build that dream together. Reassuring me when you weren't quite sure.

After my circadian cry, I climb out of bed and get the kids ready for school. When I hear the whining engine and grinding gears of the school bus fade in the distance, I turn on my computer, sit down and write one small story about my childhood. I've taped chart paper to the wall and printed, in vivid Mr. Sketch markers, fifty story starters about growing up in Kingsland. A giant-sized to-do list!

My sons are being especially kind and sympathetic. Robert gave me a tiny notebook and pen, his just-learned, jiggly cursive on the inside cover. "Dear Mom, I bought this with my own money."

They help me stay grounded and grateful.

△ △ △

IT IS THE LONG WEEKEND in May. The kids have gone on some totally fun outdoor adventure with their dad. I am home alone.

I am planting a flower garden on the sunny south side of my house. Each plant represents one strong, brave, independent woman I have known in my life. I've been planning this for weeks, reconnecting by phone or e-mail, asking each friend to choose a flower that is meaningful to them. I rely on memories for those who have died.

I plant vibrant, hardy Icelandic poppies for my grandmother Nan. Jewel-like alpine asters for my sister Kim. Bold snapdragons for my sister Robin. Cheerful cosmos for Karen. Pansies for Cheryl because "there's nothing pansy about them." Elegant white irises for Ruth. Pink carnations for my mother-in-law. Fragrant evening-scented stock for Sheila.

Mom has asked for a bleeding heart, delicate yet resilient. It languishes and droops in my sunny south bed. I consider moving it to the north side of the house, but I think it might get lonely. I tuck it behind the sunflowers selected by Robert and Michael, the only males represented in my garden.

I will call this my Courage Garden because that's what I need most. To become a woman who is not afraid to be on her own.

In July, my neighbour Tracey (of the wild auburn hair) and I decided to take our kids hiking in the mountains. Another neighbour, Peter, suggested we try the icewalk tour he guided on the Athabasca Glacier in the Columbia Ice-fields. We hatched our plans over red wine and a late-night bonfire. Tracey and I would load up our six kids, groceries and gear, and drive her truck, tent trailer and my Jeep to Jasper.

Despite a few misadventures, we climbed that glacier, trudging single file behind Peter, knapsack and pickaxe slung over his shoulder. We peered over crevasses, endlessly deep, blue and dangerous. We heard meltwater rushing down millwells. We ate Mars Bars while Peter explained glaciation in the layers of caramel and nougat. Now this was an outdoor adventure. Standing on that ground-shifting river of ice, I felt like I could do anything.

Reinvention? No. This had been inside me all along.

PART 4

{ TWELVE }

I HAVE DECIDED to go back to school.

After twenty years, I am back at the University of Alberta, standing in a long line-up on a late August afternoon to get my student ID card.

The last time I was here, no one had Rollerblades. Or cell phones. Or iPods. There was no Butterdome or campus LRT station. But those tall elm trees were here and through their yellow leaves, I can see the brown brick Dentistry building and Rutherford Library with its corniced windows. I'd always wanted to go to a university where ivy climbed up the walls.

I'm starting an interdisciplinary MA in English and Education. I am getting this third degree in every sense: the coursework is intensive and challenging—especially since I have to drive to Edmonton for weekly seminars. In snow and rain and gloom of night, just me and my red Jeep of courage.

My program will focus on creative writing. I have a great idea for my thesis.

Things haven't been the same between Mom and me since I left my marriage five years ago. Geographically and emotionally, I have become a distant daughter. I know this hurts her; we used to be so close and connected. But I've come up with a new way to bridge the distance between us.

I've arranged to meet Mom for lunch in Calgary. "There is something I'd like to run past you," I told her on the phone. I can imagine what has been running through her head.

Does she need money? Does she need to move back home? I knew she couldn't cope on her own.

I am running late, as usual. She is waiting in the entry of the Cheesecake Café. (Formerly JB's Big Boy Restaurant, where our family used to go for Mother's Day breakfasts of waffles with strawberries and whipped cream.) She is leaning slightly on her copper cane, wearing a crisp black blazer and trendy new glasses, which I duly notice. The hostess seats us in a quiet booth in the corner. I order coffee, she orders ice water. We skim the menu choices for lunch and decide on an appetizer combination to share. We make small talk until it arrives, the kind of talk my dad despises.

"How are the boys doing?"

"Good. Back to the September grind. School. Hockey."

"How is your teaching going?"

"Good. Part-time is working out okay."

"Are you still enjoying your writing? Any magazine articles I should be watching for?" She always buys several copies for me, keeping one to display on the coffee table in her living room.

"Actually, I'm not working on any magazine stuff right now. I'm kind of going in a new direction with my writing." This seems like a good segue. "In fact, I'd like to write about you."

She nearly chokes on the artichoke dip. "You've got to be kidding."

"No, I'm serious. You know that I've always been intrigued by your childhood."

She dabs the napkin to her lips, folds it on the table, smooths it with two fingers.

"My past is not particularly interesting," she says quietly.

"How can you say that? It's fascinating!" I blurt out. "Your father leaves his family in the middle of the Depression. Your mother had to find work. You had to take care of your brother and sister."

"I practically raised them."

"See? You were still a child yourself with all these adult responsibilities. And what about those unfinished adoption papers you found? Haven't you ever wondered about your real family?"

"Not really." She smooths her napkin again. "I've dealt with all the disappointments in my life."

Now it's my turn to choke. "You've got to be kidding."

"No, I'm serious. I've worked my issues." She's also picked up the jargon of self-help. Undaunted, I try another angle.

"These past few months, I've been writing about my own life, remembering my childhood and how perfect it all seemed. I've noticed these connections between the child I was and the adult I am now. I started thinking about your difficult childhood and the strong, independent woman you became. I was hoping you might share more of those stories with me."

"Why don't you ever ask me about my life now?" she asks, slightly irritated.

(The life that is displayed on the memo board on her fridge? To-do lists, calendars crammed with meetings and appointments, medication reminders, phone lists?)

"Because I want to write about your life *before* I knew you as my mother." I take a deep breath. "I want this to be my master's thesis."

I see the wrinkles on her forehead disappear. She is getting cross. I have crossed the line from private to public.

I'm hoping for *The Joy Luck Club*. She's thinking *Mommie Dearest*.

A month goes by before she finally agrees.

◊ ◊ ◊

I SCHEDULE INTERVIEWS and prepare questions, just like I used to for magazine articles. I arrange to meet Mom at pleasant tearooms with wallpaper and wainscotting. I buy a microcassette recorder and steno notepad.

My highway drives to Calgary are surprisingly calm, imbued with purpose.

I've asked Mom to gather mementos of her life before I knew her. She gives me things secular (photo albums, autograph books, newspaper articles about her teaching innovations) and things sacred (a St. Andrew daily missal, scapular on a green string and holy cards from nuns who taught her).

Mom has done some interview preparation of her own, separating her life into four chunks. The mother of all lists.

1. The Beginning: 1922–1940
2. The Teaching Years: 1941–1954; 1966–1988
3. The At-Home Years: 1955–1965
4. The Retirement Years: 1988 to present

My dad used to say that if he were to travel around the world, he would want to do it in seven days and just see the highlights. The Pyramids, the Great Wall of China, the Panama Canal…

I have the sinking feeling that Mom is doing the same with nearly eighty years of life, as though she would have preferred to skip growing up entirely, springing Athena-like as a fully formed adult.

"The Beginning" is most compelling to me and I probe for details, piecing together a childhood that seemed happy for a while. Winter sled rides on the Red River. Summers at Manitou Lake. Visits to Daddy's big office on Saturday mornings. A special outing to the Hazen-Twiss stationery store. A Waterman fountain pen just for her.

Then things began to change. Saturday evenings when she was sent to bring her father home from the Senator Hotel pub. Loud arguments waking her up at night. She would clamp a pillow over her head to muffle the sound.

Her dad lost his job. They moved into the first of many bleak houses. By this time there were two more children, a year apart. Then he disappeared entirely, enlisting for military service overseas.

"We had to move to a rundown apartment in a scummy section of town," Mom says, her eyes closed, her thoughts far away.

"I'd spend hours on my hands and knees scrubbing the dirt off the hardwood floor. At night, after I'd fed the kids and put them to bed, I would bake, trying out the recipes I'd heard on Kate Aitken's radio show. One night, the building caretaker came to the door. (Nan would have been working late at the station.) He was *exposing* himself. I slammed the door and locked it. He said he would evict us if I told."

As my mother speaks, she seems to shrink into the tearoom's paisley banquette, reliving her childhood shame.

A few weeks and interviews later, I decide that a trip to Saskatoon might inspire my writing by linking actual places with events from Mom's past. She has refused the invitation to join me.

"Why would I ever want to go back there?"

I stay at the historic Bessborough Hotel and walk along Spadina Crescent, trying to reconstruct my mother's childhood world. I stop into St. Paul's Cathedral, where beneficent stained-glass saints gaze down on me. Mom has always felt safe and comforted in church.

A few streets over, I find the apartment block where she lived when they first moved to Saskatoon from Regina. Mom would have been seven. The building is an elegant, honey-coloured ·brick, now designated an official heritage site. Mom's past has survived in spite of her.

The resident caretaker is vacuuming the red carpet. He is thin and hunched over, wearing a faded checkered shirt. Lank black hair falls across his forehead. He looks to be in his sixties. The cell phone strapped to his belt sets him squarely in the present day.

He invites me to take a look around. A graceful marble staircase leads up to the foyer and brick fireplace. Through curved archways, there are dark wooden doors with brass numbers.

I make a quick call on my phone to Mom in Calgary.

"I'm standing inside your old apartment building!"

"What on earth are you doing there?"

"Primary research! Which number did you live in?"

There is a pause.

"B-11," she says. "God knows how I remembered that."

"B-11 has a tenant," the caretaker tells me, "but you can take a look at my place, if you don't mind the mess."

He points out relics from the past. The kitchen cupboards, eating nook (See how the benches lift up?) and plaster ceilings are original. Same with the hardwood floors, linoleum and countertop tiles. A framed portrait of Princess Diana hangs on the kitchen wall. School photos (grandchildren?) sit beside an overflowing ashtray on top of the TV. I take his word on the original bedroom fixtures when I glimpse the *Hustler* calendar pinned above the headboard.

I try to imagine my mother, my grandmother Nan, and the grandfather I never knew in their apartment in 1933. Did Nan wear bright red lipstick and smoke Du Mauriers back then? Mom says her father was Jimmy Stewart handsome—slim and tall with brown eyes and thick dark hair.

This was the last place they were together as a family.

"The laundry room is real old," says the caretaker. We follow the smell of fabric softener through a cramped basement hallway. Two steel washtubs are flanked by newer appliances along the wall. (Was I expecting washboards and wringer washers?) A clothesline spans the length of the room beneath brown water stains on the ceiling. The afternoon light is grey through the high, narrow window.

Another hallway leads to the storage room, damp and smelling of mildew. A row of wooden lockers with metal hasps and white stencilled numbers line the far wall. Bicycles and bed frames lean beside them. A brass-bound steamer trunk, just like one at Mom's house, sits in the corner.

"I'll show you the furnace room."

Fire dances and hisses in a huge steel drum that takes up all the space. The boiler hangs above; yellow asbestos leaks out of a gash.

"I call this my workshop," he laughs. A wiry Hephaestus in his dungeon of metal and heat. Or a Bluebeard. Killing curious wives and hiding their corpses in dark, subterranean chambers.

One thing is true. In this apartment building, I have found the remains of my mother's lost childhood.

△ △ △

I RETURN FROM SASKATOON feeling elated. I phone Mom to share my sleuthing discoveries.

"Hello, dear. How was your trip?"

I hear her raspy voice, hacking cough. I can imagine the rest: chest pain, aching ribs, fitful sleeps.

"It's just a sore throat," she assures me. "All I need is a good night's rest. Nothing to worry about."

This is worrisome. Mom's physical health has continued to deteriorate. The potent painkillers in her medicine cabinet are vying for shelf space with steroids for chronic bronchitis and beta blockers for heart arrhythmia.

On the third day, she feels wretched and agrees to see a doctor. Some nice young man at a walk-in clinic who sends her home with an arsenal of sinus sprays, inhalers, antibiotics and reassurance. "If you were my mother, this is what I would recommend."

There is no one left of the doctors who really knew her. She smooths Vicks VapoRub on her chest, wraps a wool sock around her neck and climbs into bed.

On the seventh day, Dad calls an ambulance. Mom, weak, dehydrated and disoriented, puts on her scratchy tartan wool robe and offers to make tea for the paramedics. They take her to the hospital instead.

For my mother, just a sore throat can be dangerous.

△ △ △

THERE ARE NO pleasant tearooms on this visit to Calgary. I go straight to the Rockyview hospital, ascending from parkade gloom into the bright white glare of another Cardiac Intensive Care Unit.

It's ironic. No sooner does Dad's heart get fixed than Mom's goes haywire. A CICU tag team.

She is resting in a bed flanked by monitors and IV poles. Get-well cards and teddy bears crowd the bedside table. Her eyes open when she hears my footsteps.

I navigate through tubes and wires to give her a kiss. My lips brush against parchment.

Mom introduces me as "Daughter Number Three" to the day nurse.

"Your mother has been a saint," she tells me. "Never complains. Even with all that poking and prodding from the doctors."

Lung Man. Heart Man. G-I Man. Mom's retinue of superhero specialists. They've agreed, finally, that the antibiotics have reacted with her heart drugs in some sort of toxic cocktail.

"The doctors have never seen anything like this," Mom tells me. "They want to write it up in a medical journal."

She seems flattered. This is a story she likes.

My story will have to wait.

In the meantime, Mom will have rest, radical new drugs and round-the-clock care at her own version of Club Med.

I kept chipping away at my research, creating timelines and transcripts of Mom's life from our interviews. I looked at her photos again and reread the inscriptions on holy cards from nuns, urging her to pray to Mary and persevere.

She persevered all right. She developed a will of iron.

As a child, my mother faced real fears she had to overcome all by herself. I had a safe, secure childhood but was scared to do anything alone. Patterns of behaviour that had followed me well into adulthood.

Was this the way my mother willed it?

◇ ◇ ◇

ON OTHER MATTERS of the heart, my Swiss Guide and I are finally on solid, common ground, after time spent apart on our separate paths. We decide to get engaged, the actual marriage pending completion of obligatory annulments and construction of a new home for our special family blend. If my first wedding was all about shortcuts, this second one is taking the long way around. Which suits us both fine.

Which is not to say I don't have plans.

I've been holding on to a *Good Housekeeping* article from 1998 called "The Second Time Around." Part inspiration, part talisman, its pages are creased and torn. The writer tells how she found love again after her divorce. As a couple they were committed to each other, but children and ex-spouses complicated things. The article ends with a tender description of the wedding ceremony.

We both have our moments of second-guessing this second marriage; it's hard to give up our independence and single-parent routines even though we want to be together. I need to safeguard my writing space. I only want to teach part-time. He supports this completely. He needs to safeguard his time with his son. My kids will be spending more time with us than his. Will that cause resentment? Will everyone get along? We've both heard the horror stories about blending families. We fret, we talk, we hope for the best.

Eventually, we decide on a Saturday in early February for the wedding. Groundhog Day. Whether this symbolizes hope for an early spring (as in the time-worn tradition) or another chance to get things right (as in the 1993 movie), this day bodes well for a celebration. It is also my Swiss Guide's—Gerald's—birthday. Robert draws a kooky cartoon for the invitation. I find the perfect dress (an iridescent scarlet silk) while power-shopping between hockey games at a weekend tournament. We have booked a hall for a casual reception with a camping theme, complete with lanterns, checkered tablecloths and plastic bugs. There will be a dinner and dance and silliness with garters and bouquets. A big party for everyone.

Except for my parents. Dad has no interest in attending—one wedding per daughter was enough for him—and Mom is still struggling with her heart issues. Seems the new wonder drug hasn't been so wonderful after all. A week before the wedding, she's back in the hospital.

Mom tells me how disappointed she is that she can't be there. She was *so* looking forward to the ceremony and reception and meeting my new family. Still, I can't help feeling like her absence is a kind of boycott. I've planned this new phase of my life without falling apart or even asking her advice (which seems appropriate at forty-two) but am I breaking her heart in the process?

△ △ △

MARRIAGE.

That was the topic of the sermon at this wedding.

The priest, a gifted orator, had agreed to my request to weave the words of poet Rainer Maria Rilke into his homily, a paraphrasing from *Letters to a Young Poet* that captured our best hopes. "Marriage is not a matter of creating a quick community of spirit by tearing down and destroying all boundaries. Once the realization is accepted that even between the closest people infinite distances exist, a marvellous living side by side can grow up, if they succeed in loving the distance between them no less than one another."

While these heartfelt words were being spoken, my mother was climbing out of her hospital bed and collapsing onto the floor.

I didn't know this at the time, of course, but I do remember a sudden feeling of constriction and breathlessness as I stood before the altar. A flutter of anxiety.

Wedding jitters, I told myself, and held on tightly to my new husband's hand.

Meanwhile, Mom was being resuscitated on a code blue call, mercifully pulled back from some liminal brink where she remembers walking through the hospital walls to a drugstore soda fountain in Saskatoon.

A few days after our wedding, we visit Mom in the hospital, bringing flowers, photos and a piece of cake. She enjoys the stories we share about the day, apologizes again for missing it. She tells us the doctors have decided that a pacemaker will be the best fix for her heart. When she is stronger, they will hook her up.

On the day of Mom's pacemaker insertion five months later, I am three hundred kilometres away in the Rutherford Library, finishing my thesis.

It was supposed to be about my mother's childhood but kept defaulting to mine.

There are a couple reasons for this. I remember practically everything about my own childhood and can't stop writing about it. And Mom (health issues notwithstanding) doesn't really want to remember, much less talk about, hers. "I don't like going back to those places," she told me. "The feelings of sadness get stuck in my throat."

This thesis was supposed to be a new way to connect with my mother. Adult to adult. I'd wanted to show my love and admiration by writing the story of her life. In truth, I think Mom has resented me rummaging around in her past, neglecting her present self. She prefers our old way of connecting through crisis. But I don't want to be that needy child anymore.

As sunlight streams through the library windows, I type myself a note.

When my mother is asleep and her heart is open, I will reach in and grab the child she keeps locked there for safekeeping. To fill the empty space, I will leave these stories of my wonder-filled childhood.

Ctrl-S.

The pacemaker operation is a success. Mom gets stronger and healthier. She resumes her busy life of homemaking, volunteering and *Gran*-mothering. Dad needs even more of her time now.

I give Mom a Cerlox-bound copy of my thesis for Christmas. "You must be so pleased to be finished," she says.

I am. And in the process of writing it, I have found a place where I can be calmly, joyfully, absolutely alone.

There is no need for rescue.

{ THIRTEEN }

IT IS NIGHTTIME and I am asleep. A thick, instant sleep at the end of a hectic day. Suddenly I sit bolt upright. Coughing, sputtering, gasping. I catch my breath. Clear my throat.

I lie down again. Try to go back to sleep.

That was weird. Was I dreaming? Why was I choking? I swallow slowly, cautiously.

Why was I choking?

I take calming breaths. Breathe in, two, three, and out, two, three.

What if I choke to death?

I tense my legs. Hold. Relax. Tense my arms. Hold. Relax. Tense my shoulders. Hold. Relax. This uncomfortable feeling will pass.

I start to shiver uncontrollably beneath the blankets.

I am alone in our house.

And newly afraid.

◌ ◌ ◌

IT HAS BEEN four years since I bought my first anxiety workbook.

I have learned about the gestalt of anxiety, its blend of heredity, upbringing and cumulative stress. I recognize the personality traits that perpetuate anxiety—perfectionism, a need for approval and control—as well as a tendency to ignore physical symptoms of stress: headaches, stomach ache, sleeping problems.

I have filled in checklists and answered questionnaires. I fall into the mild-to-moderate range of anxious, which can be managed through good nutrition, regular aerobic activity, deep muscle relaxation, positive self-talk and honouring my inner child.

My bookshelves are filled with slim volumes on reducing stress, embracing uncertainty and awakening intuition. I have visited websites and downloaded files.

I've become something of an armchair expert on anxiety. I've got it handled.

So this throat thing must be something else.

No longer self-conscious in the bookstore's self-help section, I scan the titles, my neck bent sideways, looking for the quintessential resource like *A Doctor Talks to 40-to-45-Year-Olds,* or something along those lines.

Evidently, this lump-in-the-throat sensation is called *globus hystericus* in Latin, a particularly female complaint once believed to be caused by a wandering uterus.

Great. A hormonal harbinger of perimenopause. A midlife musical reprise of "I Enjoy Being a Girl."

Or is it a thyroid problem?

A vitamin B12 deficiency?

Hyperglycemia?

Hypoglycemia?

Anemia?

Can a person actually choke to death on phlegm? (A recent string of movies with consumptive female leads has me worried. *Moulin Rouge. Finding Neverland.*)

I ask my family doctor about this, casually, during a routine checkup. She tries hard not to smile.

I smile, too. Wascally pwe-menopausal wabbit.

Then I get a sore throat. The kind that usually leads to a head cold.

I take extra vitamin C, a couple Aspirins and go to bed. A good night's rest is all I need.

The first night, no sleep.

No problem.

I've learned how to manage the odd restless night with good sleep-hygiene habits. Get up. Gargle with salt water.

Do a full-body relaxation. Write in my notebook. Contemplate the basket of ironing and a stack of student essays. Go back to bed.

Call in sick to work the next day.

Second night. No sleep again. Fatigue and phlegm are pooled in every cell of my body.

I go to the walk-in clinic the next morning.

"Throat's a little red. Lungs sound clear. Just a virus. Get some rest."

No problem.

Third night. No sleep.

I'm sick and exhausted. Wide awake on a dextromethorphan buzz. Alone in the house. A perfect alchemy for awfulizing in the deep, still darkness of three a.m.

So this is it.

My nervous breakdown has arrived. I am not in a housedress shaking on the kitchen floor. I am not running, wild-eyed, out onto the street. I am lying in my bed, mortally congested, feeling a dreamlike sensation of falling.

Off the ladder of the Blue Imp slide.

Over guardrails into roaring spillways.

In cars coasting backwards down steep hills.

Inside the lurching elevator of Calgary's old Eaton's store...

Daylight streams through elegant glass doors, then disappears behind solid metal slabs. The elevator attendant pulls the clattering gate across with her white-gloved hand, sits primly on the stool and cranks the brass handle. Invisible pulleys whir and hum, hoisting us upward.

"Second Floor: ladies wear, millinery, shoes." Sunshine floods back through the glass doors. "Third floor: home furnishings, china, carpets."

"Going down."

We fall toward the basement.

Twisted ropes of steel pay out,

Snapping taut . . .

"Stop!" I yell out loud, sitting up in bed, gripping the sides of my head with my hands, trying to squeeze the image out.

Why can't I sleep? Why can't I get better? What am I doing wrong?

On cue, my personal Greek Chorus, gossamer-robed, glides in and assembles in the corners of my room, stage-whispering their cautions:

Hubris.

Who do you think you are?

Nemesis.

This is what you deserve.

Anxious by day, sleepless by night. A comeuppance of mythic proportions. Even Prometheus had a chance to regroup each night.

This is what you deserve.

But my life is not a Greek tragedy.

I am forty-five years old. I teach half-time and write, still searching for that balance between pursuing art and paying bills. Lately, my teaching job has been bringing me down. Gerald is talking about changing careers: he feels restless.

My sons, now thirteen and sixteen, are healthy, normal, self-absorbed teenagers. My stepson, Matt, is ten, slightly spoiled. Marriage, the second attempt, is going okay. Together we are exploring this rugged new territory called "The Blended Family." Rocks and roots of resentment, steep slopes of second thoughts, crevices of guilt. But every so often, the sun breaks through the mist on distant peaks. Like on our recent family trip to Disneyland: the Happiest Place on Earth—except for that incident with the teacups.

(I was determined to do one thing at Disneyland: ride in those teacups that twirled on *The Wonderful World of Disney* every Sunday night of my childhood. My teenage sons want no part of this spin down memory lane with their mother. My husband agrees to go with me and as we walk through the throng of people and strollers, we realize this is the first time in days we've been alone together. We hold hands.

"Dad, wait up! I want to come, too." Behind us, Matt is running to catch up.

"We're going by ourselves," I whisper to Gerald, digging my nails into his palm.

"We'll be back in a little while," he reassures his son. "Okay, bud?" He watches him walk back through the crowd, dejected, his little knapsack dragging on the ground. Feeling more Queen of Hearts than Alice in Wonderland, I twirl relentlessly in a purple teacup opposite my Mock Turtle husband.)

The real-life drama is with my parents, now into their eighties. Mom has to will herself to stay well so she can take care of Dad, who seems to have lost interest in life. He eats very little and sleeps a lot.

Why can't I sleep?

I do what I often do in these fearful nights filled with questions: I phone a friend for the answer. My sister; my lifeline. It's becoming more of a habit, these late-night calls to Kim when I can't sleep. By day, this dependency bothers me. By night, I am desperate for a fix.

Her voice is groggy and thick on the other end of the phone.

"Hello?"

"Sorry to wake you. I just had this really scary feeling like I was trapped in the elevator in the old Eaton's store, falling to the basement out of control—"

"You're doing this to yourself."

Her voice gets stronger. She's in control now. "Stop thinking negative thoughts."

"I can't."

"Yes, you can. Say this: 'I am calm and at peace.'"

"I am calm and at peace. Am I losing my mind?"

"No. You've just got a lot on your mind."

I am too afraid to hang up. To be alone in the darkness with dread-filled thoughts. My sister says she will stay on the phone. We will stay connected. A benediction for my sleep through a sacrifice of hers.

(Benediction and sacrifice. Two words my sister would rather crucify me with than have associated with her. She who had scored one hundred percent on the Bishop's Exam of Catechism in grade three, she who had dutifully fasted and fainted during High Mass, she who had read *The Nun's Story* ten times—imagining herself doing God's work in the Congo—had ditched on being Catholic. Maybe out of respect for my father's skepticism, maybe out of disdain for my mother's stoicism, Kim explored alternative philosophies voraciously. Meditation, reiki, crystals, tarot cards, astrology. She devoured books by Louise Hay and Caroline Myss. She was so knowledgeable, passionate and older-sister-bossy that I'd become her disciple.)

"You need some time to work things out," she tells me. "Why don't you just put down your end of the skipping rope? You're like an ever-ender. You keep turning and turning because someone on the other end tells you to."

"I never get to jump in and play?"

"Or rest. You need to ask for some time off work."

No. Campbells don't take those kinds of leaves. We let ourselves go to the edge with insomnia, pneumonia and heart arrhythmia instead. I once made the mistake of telling Dad I took a "mental health" day off from teaching. "You don't look sick to me," he said, his eyes burning holes into my flimsy character.

"I took a stress leave," Kim reminds me. It was over ten years ago. She was working full-time for an oil company, had a three-year-old son and a generally unhelpful husband. "One Sunday afternoon, I began to feel all spacey and edgy. I couldn't breathe. My heart was racing. I was breaking out in hives. So I drove to Emergency."

"By yourself?" I am impressed by this detail alone. "What was wrong?"

"I was having a panic attack. The psychiatrist on call wrote me a prescription."

This is news to me. My sister never *ever* takes medication.

"What was it for?"

"Two weeks off work. It saved me."

The next day, I request a medical leave from teaching. I am going to rest, walk and write my way back to health.

My family doctor is unconvinced. "I'm worried about you. Physically *and* mentally. You're stressed at work, raising teenagers, worried about your parents. You seem really sad."

I sense where she's going with this.

"I don't need any medication. I just need a couple weeks to regroup. I'll be okay."

"I want to see you again in two weeks."

Maybe my problem needs younger guns.

Or guns that don't know me at all.

⌂ ⌂ ⌂

MY CHAIN VISITS to walk-in clinics begin. I am a generic patient sitting in a generic waiting room, my ailments increasing with every stale-dated magazine I flip through. Could I have non-Hodgkin's lymphoma? Acid reflux? My symptoms seem to match:

1. sore throat and cough
2. heartburn
3. stomach pain
4. sleeping problems

Papers fly off the doctors' prescription pads. I fold them into my hand like so many origami birds.

The pills lined up in my medicine cabinet have names like space aliens. Biaxin. Prevacid. Zopiclone. I am afraid to take any of them for any amount of time, having read the warning labels: diarrhea, dyspepsia, dependency.

Which brings me to this moment with Doctor Number 11 at Walk-In Clinic Number 4.

"I'll tell you what your problem is," says the young doctor, his brown eyes serious behind glasses rimmed in silver rectangles. His longish dark hair is swept back, grazing the collar of his white coat. His head and shoulders are framed by certificates and graduate photos from distant medical schools.

I sit across from him on the edge of the examining table. Pissed off at my body. Again. Off on some spur line without my permission. Again. This is the eleventh doctor I have consulted over the past two months at four different walk-in clinics. I have seen doctors ranging in age from Doogie Howser to Marcus Welby in search of an explanation.

"I'll tell you *exactly* what your problem is," he says again, leaning back on his chair, crossing his legs and linking his fingers across his knee. "You have G.A.D."

(*Gad?* To go about idly or in search of pleasure?)

"It stands for generalized anxiety disorder. You have a serious problem."

He takes out his prescription pad. Scrawls the name of a new space alien.

"Celexa. It's an antidepressant."

I'm not depressed, I tell him. I'm *physically* ill.

(Besides, my practice of flushing mood-altering pharmaceuticals down the toilet has become an act of personal power, although not particularly good for the environment.)

"This SSRI is effective for anxiety as well as depression. Very few side effects." He makes a zero with his thumb and index finger.

I don't need medication, I tell him again, I have my anxiety handled.

(Besides, I fall into the mild-to-moderate range of anxious, which can be managed through good nutrition, regular aerobic activity, deep muscle relaxation, positive self-talk and...)

"But you *don't* have it handled. You're not sleeping. You're not working. You're obsessing about your health."

Could this be acid reflux? I interrupt. An ulcer?

"No! You have a chemical imbalance in your brain that is causing you to be anxious most of the time. You need medication immediately. Maybe permanently."

No, not that. Please.

I look down at the floor. Grey-and-white-speckled linoleum. Tears pool on the rims of my glasses.

He stands up and gently touches my arm, waits for me to look at him. His brown eyes are gentle.

"Would you judge someone with diabetes who took insulin? Do you think I'm a weak person because I take pills for high blood pressure?"

"Of course not," I answer. "That's not your fault."

"This isn't your fault either."

Later, I crumple and burn his prescription. I bury the charred remains beneath the snow in my front garden, scrabbling through layers of frozen leaves and soil. My hands are black with ash.

I don't need antidepressants. Now or ever.

△ △ △

I GO SEE a naturopath instead.

This doctor is the youngest one yet, soft-spoken and calm. She performs a thorough examination and, a week later, meets with me to discuss the protocol. I will need to cleanse from candida yeast. Change my diet. Drink more water. Massage acupressure points. Practise visualization.

"You can learn how to heal your body," she tells me.

"So I'm not going crazy?"

"No. You're not going crazy."

I am so relieved that I hug her.

My first order of naturopathic business, along with the yeast cleanse, is to stop taking zopiclone, a turquoise oval that makes sleep fall swiftly and surely, like the final curtain after a concert. I was deathly afraid to take it in the first place, remembering those hazy Halcion days of twenty years before. I asked a girlfriend to stay with me the first night, since my husband was out of town. She sat in the living room reading a magazine until I slept. On the second night, I asked Robert to stay with me.

"I'm going out," he says. "I have a life, you know."

"But I really need you to stay. Just for a little while. Until I fall asleep. I have to take this pill because I haven't been sleeping very well and it scares me."

He grudgingly agrees. I think he's a little scared himself.

I take half a pill and crawl into bed. Robert is slouched on the loveseat across the bedroom, arms crossed, plugged into his iPod. Sound hisses out of his earphones.

"What are you listening to?" I have to practically yell the question.

"Avenged Sevenfold," he yells back.

"Sounds soothing."

I begin to feel drowsy and relaxed.

"Thanks, Rob. I'm okay now. You can go."

The original plan was to take zopiclone for a few days to "break the cycle" of insomnia. Three weeks later, I can't sleep without it. My naturopath has given me dire warnings about the stuff and I am eager to be free of it. She gives me some homeopathic tinctures to help me get through the next few nights, since there may be a "rebound effect."

The first night was filled with horrific technicolour dreams. I am searching for my son Robert. I find him in a van with a bunch of rock band junkies. I peer through blue haze to find him. He has long scraggly hair and is smoking crack cocaine. The second night, cockroaches and scorpions scuttle up and around a blue toilet covered in weeds and thick vines.

I remember comparing my detox experience to that of old Mrs. Dubose in *To Kill a Mockingbird*. She weans herself from a morphine dependency to die free, unbeholden to anyone or anything. Atticus Finch tells his children that Mrs. Dubose showed true courage even though she was mean and crotchety. I am being courageous, too. Not wanting to depend on medication.

But I still can't sleep.

The naturopath answers my desperate late-night phone calls. Add lavender to your bathwater, she says. Take melatonin before bed. Put gemstones under your pillow.

I can heal my body.

Sister Kim remains the biggest booster for my holistic "Just Say No" approach, quoting chapter and verse from the Internet on the evils of all the medications I have been prescribed. "Biaxin destroys your stomach lining and increases anxiety. Zopliclone is habit-forming and worsens depression. Allopathic medicines are toxic!"

I am afraid to listen. I am afraid not to listen.

She would have been great in the Congo.

◊ ◊ ◊

IT IS NEARLY three months into my two-week stress leave.

I dread getting up each morning to face a day where I've lost all sense of routine and purpose. I'm not teaching. I'm not writing. Cleaning my messy house would be a practical choice—maybe even therapeutic—but I'm exhausted and don't give a shit.

"Just do one thing," my mother used to say.

I dust the silk plants.

I have no attention span to read a book or even watch a movie. And every time I try, the story is about someone struggling with mental illness—*White Oleander*, *Matchstick Men*... Even a usually pleasant experience, like getting my hair cut, is uncomfortable. The chemicals smell too strong. The music is too loud. I'm shivering under the black nylon cape. And *O, The Oprah Magazine* I'm attempting to read has a feature on antidepressants. Skip that.

I have no appetite. I make myself eat plain yogurt.

Driving is out. At least anything further than a few blocks. Stoplights make me tense. I feel trapped in traffic jams.

My sons are mystified and pissed off. Their mother stays at home, wears ratty old sweats and lies in bed all the time. But she doesn't look sick. She snaps when they ask for simple things like having friends over or getting a ride to the mall. She can't drive them to their volleyball tournaments in Calgary or Edmonton like she used to. They know something is wrong—she cries for no reason and hugs them more than usual—but no one seems to be talking.

My husband is supportive but equally mystified. This anxiety that comes from daily living just doesn't make sense to him. Mountain climbing? Maybe. Bear attacks? Absolutely. But driving around the city? Shopping at Costco? Missing Dwight Yoakam in concert?

True to his Swiss guide sensibilities, Gerald tries to steady me on this shaky ground. He comes home from work in the middle of the day, makes me healthy salads and herbal teas, holds me through tearful, terror-filled nights, but he cannot keep me from falling.

The only thing I do well is walk. Twice a day, in any weather. At least my legs, lungs and heart are working, although my stomach feels like it's falling out and my esophagus is on fire. I usually walk alone but prefer going with a friend. Just to keep the scary thoughts from buzzing around the front of my brain—or in case I collapse on the path. There are two golden retrievers on my walking route. They bound over to see me every day, barking and smiling. I squeeze my hand through the chain-link fence to scratch their ears and pet them. They seem to know I'm going through a tough time and are trying to cheer me up.

I go to bed every night by nine, but I don't sleep much. Fading in and out, suddenly wakeful, soaked with sweat, the bedclothes twisted around me. If I could just get my sleep back, I know I'd be fine.

I add reiki massage to my health regimen.

And hypnotherapy.

I consider acupuncture.

I buy a meditation CD and feel the sensation of hot lava rise in my throat with every in-breath.

A friend gives me a silky soft teddy bear named Kumo "for courage and strength."

I make a snow angel in the deep drifts of the backyard. Lying on my back, sun warming my face, I breathe deeply, calmly, white puffs of vapour rising from my mouth. I squint up at the clear blue sky.

Please help me get well.

Whenever I was afraid as a child, I prayed to a gentle, golden-haired Jesus like the one in the Sacred Heart of Jesus painting in my mother-in-law's guest room. Now all I can relate to is the burning heart. I don't pray much anymore, still a victim of my own original sins. But I wish I could find that comfort again. That feeling of love and support beyond myself.

Maybe it's time for Confession. For real.

The priest shakes my hand as we introduce ourselves. He is a few years younger than me, which is unusual, but okay. He is post-Act of Contrition.

He sits behind his desk, drapes a purple stole around his neck, and we proceed.

"Father, forgive me, for I have sinned. It's been fifteen, uh, twenty years since my last Confession. These are my sins..."

Afterward, the priest explains how the sacrament—now called "Reconciliation"—allows healing to begin. "I tell schoolchildren that it's like an Etch-a-Sketch. Their sins are magically erased."

I smile. Metaphorically speaking, we are soulmates, he and I.

And as I leave the church, the sun breaks through the clouds. Faith renewed, sins forgiven, my health is miraculously restored.

Alleluia. Amen.

But that would be a lie.

△ △ △

SUDDENLY, MICHAEL DOESN'T WANT to go to school. He's had a falling-out with his friends and it has been getting progressively worse. Teasing. Taunts. Threats. One morning, he is curled up on his bed, clutching his stomach. "I can't go. I feel like throwing up."

My own stomach drops. "You have to go to school."

"You don't have to go to work. Why can't I stay here with you?"

"Because you can't. Besides, I'm sick."

"What are you sick with?"

"Mononucleosis. You know that."

This part was true. I did have a positive mono test weeks ago. This was the public story we gave friends and relatives when they noticed I'd dropped out of sight.

"I wish I had mono," Michael says, absently stroking Kumo's fuzzy paw.

I'm trying to appear calm, but my heart and mind are racing. Is my anxiety contagious? Hereditary? Why is this fun-loving, outgoing, confident kid suddenly afraid to go to school?

I wish I had the magical powers now. I'd give him the confidence to go back to school. I'd zap those bullying little jerks in the process.

I search for some sort of wisdom and advice.

"Listen. If you don't go to school today, it will only get harder and harder to go back. You can get through this."

I give him a silver-grey metallic gemstone to put in his pocket. "It's hematite. For courage."

I drive him to school. If he only knew how much courage that took.

"It's weird," Michael says as he slowly opens the car door, "I don't want to go to school, but I have to. You want to go to school, but you can't."

"You're right. It's weird."

"It's *ironic*," he says, trying hard not to smile.

I wonder if I should be telling my kids more about my health problem—whatever it is. Super-mono-anxious-listless-expialidocious. I've been keeping it from my ex-husband, too. I can't show any weakness. I'm afraid he will blame me for not being a good mother, or worse, for causing this problem in our youngest son.

I remember a teacher who took a medical leave a few years earlier. Once the big fears were ruled out (cancer, heart disease), our staff speculated about what the problem could be. Stress? Nervous breakdown? He was candid on his return. He told us he'd been diagnosed with clinical depression. "I'm not ashamed anymore to admit that," he told us. "My own children need to know this about me. Depression might be part of their lives, too. I want them to know the signs and know there's help."

I remember admiring his honesty. This wonderful father and teacher, poleaxed by errant brain function.

What if that was happening to me?

△ △ △

MY HUSBAND BOOKS a trip to Palm Springs over spring break. Just the two of us. A change of scene and the desert air might just be the cure, he tells me. I can read and relax by the pool, shop at the factory outlets and walk in warm sunshine after our dismal winter of grey skies and fog.

I am afraid to go.

The flight is smooth across blue skies. Gerald reaches across me to point out the Great Salt Lake, Grand Canyon, Mojave Desert. His tour continues from our rental car. "There's Mount San Jacinto, Bob Hope's house, Bing Crosby's trailer park..."

I am keeping track of where the hospitals are.

We pick up some groceries and I tag along behind like a little kid, afraid to get separated in the long aisles of strangers speaking Spanish. I can't bear to have him out of my sight, here in this new place. By the next day, he's had just about enough when I insist that he eat his Del Taco lunch in the car. I can't handle going into the crowded restaurant.

"I hate eating in the car!" he yells as shredded lettuce spills onto his shorts, taco sauce drips down his fingers. He jabs at the mess with a napkin. "Why can't we just eat in the restaurant like normal people?"

It's the "normal" that sets me off. I start to cry. Gerald feels bad and we spend some time in a New Age bookstore downtown. I buy *You Can Heal Your Life* by Louise Hay and a blank journal titled "Destiny." He buys me a lavender crystal. "It says amethyst is a natural tranquilizer," he says, reading from the chart. "Apparently, it 'soothes stress, dispels anxiety and relieves insomnia.' Do you think it might work by tonight so I can go to the casino?" he jokes.

I don't think it's funny. He knows I'm scared to be alone in a new city.

He sighs. "I just don't understand what you're afraid of."

My problem is way more than he's gambled for.

◊ ◊ ◊

AS WE DRIVE BACK to our place, I try to explain the sensation of anxiety to him with this memory.

When I was around four, I went to the Calgary Stampede for the very first time. I had a new cowboy hat with a whistle. Mom wore yellow stretchy pants and Dad wore his string tie. "Hold on tight to my hand," said my mom as we moved toward the crowded midway.

I heard the *click-click-click* of the roller coaster climbing, the screams as it clattered down, the music of the merry-go-round and the shouts of rough men to come and play, try your luck, win a prize. I watched a stout lady, her arms red and damp, spinning sugar-pink clouds of candy floss. Almost sick with excitement, I reached for my mother's hand.

Someone else's mother looked down at me.

I whirled around. The legs of strangers engulfed me.

"Mom!" I shrieked.

She was only a short distance away—thank God for yellow pants—but I have never forgotten those seconds of terror.

And *that's* what my adult anxiety feels like. A child lost and alone. And no matter how much I rationalize it ("You're a grown woman. You've done this before. There is nothing to be afraid of."), those physical sensations of fear won't stop. Like a record-player needle skidding at the end of an old LP.

Gerald is silent for a while. "I wish I could help you more."

"You are helping. You've been really patient. It's been a tough three months."

"Would you be okay here if I went out to play cards for a couple hours?" he asks tentatively. The Augustine Casino shines like a beacon in the desert. He deserves a break from me.

"I'll try."

It is dusk. Sitting in a lounge chair in the safe confines of the Desert Aire RV Resort, surrounded by steadfast, reliable seniors, I read my new book and repeat the affirmations: "I love and approve of myself. I am willing to release the pattern in me that is creating this condition."

This feels silly. Hopeless. Like reading a book on how to swim while I'm drowning.

I look up at the stars in the darkening sky, searching, begging, "God? I need help. Nothing is working."

Silence. Then sputtering. Automatic sprinklers rise up from the ground, blasting water over me in a cool, redemptive spray.

◊ ◊ ◊

I DECIDE TO RETURN to work after spring break. Just to have the routine and interaction with people back and, mostly, to get my mind off my mind. I've been off for three months, after all. I should be a little better by now.

(Besides, I'm not sick enough for a long-term disability leave. Maybe if I had cancer, something really serious. Nor do I want to fill out all the forms, have soul-baring phone conversations with faceless benefit-plan officers. Most of all, I don't want to see a psychiatrist.)

I manage the first day of work. Shivering, arms wrapped around my sides like a straitjacket, I have trouble concentrating on the assignments stacked up for marking. I try to act back-to-normal for the students who drift in and out of the Outreach school.

"Hey, you're back! Heard you had mono. Sucks, doesn't it?"

"Totally."

"Wow. You've lost a lot of weight," remarks another.

"Yeah." My rapid weight loss has been frightening—like a disappearing act.

On the third day, I am hiding out in the staff washroom.

"I'm not doing very well," I confess to a colleague who follows me in.

"I noticed." She leans against the wall behind me as I splash cold water on my face. She talks to my reflection in the mirror. "I know what you're going through."

This is where forgiveness begins.

FOURTEEN

T HERE'S ONE CHAPTER in my anxiety workbook that I have always skipped. The one
called "Medications." I've been too scared to read it.

I return to it now, made a little braver by someone
else's story.

Once again, my anxiety book seems to hold up a mirror.

Apart from your personal values, the next thing to look
at in considering medication is the severity of your symp-
toms... Use the following questions to evaluate the severity of
your own condition...

Does your anxiety significantly interfere with your ability to function in your everyday life?

Yes.

Are you having a hard time working or are you unable to work at all?

Yes.

Is your ability to raise your children or be responsive to your spouse impaired by your anxiety?

Yes.

Does your problem with anxiety cause you considerable distress to the point where you have two or more hours every day where you feel very uncomfortable?

Yes.

Do you wake up each morning in a state of dread?

Yes.

Shit.

I am no longer mild or moderate. I am severely anxious.

The real question to ask is . . . what is the most compassionate thing you can do for yourself?

Somewhere inside me, a calm voice responds: Try the antidepressants.

I return to my family doctor. Same examining room as the last time we spoke, eleven doctors ago. The Norman Rockwell calendar on the wall is flipped to April.

"I hope you won't say, 'I told you so.'" I quip, then burst into tears.

She doesn't.

◊ ◊ ◊

EACH MORNING, I sit on my sunny front porch drinking peppermint tea, waiting anxiously to feel better. I walk a lot. Write a little.

My mother used to tell the story of the day Kim got her first pair of glasses. She was only three. After they got home, Kim came racing in from the TV room, shouting, "Mommy, Mommy! Howdy Doody has a face!"

I wish antidepressants worked that quickly.

I could crawl out of my skin with restless boredom. It feels like every single Good Friday service I sat through as a child has been strung together in one beatifically boring chunk.

How ironic that on this particular Good Friday, I am sitting in the hospital emergency ward, convinced that Celexa (day ten) is making me worse. I feel edgier than ever, sick to my stomach and I'm still not sleeping.

I wait in a windowless room with a black vinyl couch, stained carpet and beige walls with a couple holes punched in by someone's angry fist. Three hours later, the doctor arrives, apologizing for the Good Friday backlog. He sits beside me and we talk for a long time.

"You're not losing your mind," he assures me. "Just be patient."

(I wish he would admit me so I could *be* a patient, resting undisturbed under cool white sheets, until I got well.)

He prescribes Ativan for anxiety. Zopiclone for zees.

"And quit thinking so much," he says, patting my shoulder. "Smile!"

I keep meticulous track of every single pill I take on every single day, waiting for that magic four-to-six-week mark when I should begin to feel... what? Calm? Happy? Antidepressed?

Just be patient.

So I work on little daily projects, like stripping and staining the teak patio furniture, my mind racing out ahead. *Why isn't this medication working? What if you're getting worse? Why don't you take a few swigs of linseed oil and end it all right here?*

I clean up the winter debris in my flower garden: dead leaves, stray newspapers, Cellophane wrappers. I find pieces of charred prescription paper, damp and dirty, slightly decomposed. A tenacious little artifact from my Denial Period.

I spend hours on the phone—like some crisis-hotline caller—talking to a few close friends. These conversation balloons tether me to the present, keep me from drifting into wide-open skies of what-if.

Even my ex-husband has been kind and compassionate. I'd finally broken down and told him. We'd been watching Robert's volleyball game together. I'd been trying to act like a normal spectator, chatting and cheering. I'd consumed half a pack of Halls honey lemon lozenges to keep my mind off choking to death.

By the end of the match, I was hyperventilating.

"Can we talk?" I asked him between lemony menthol breaths. "Can you come over for a beer?"

"Okay," he says hesitantly. This is an unusual invitation. "I'll be there in half an hour."

This is the first time he's been past the front entryway of my house. We sit in the backyard on the newly restained patio chairs. He takes a sip of his beer. I have another Halls.

"I've been having a hard time these last few months," I begin, faltering.

"Yeah, the kids have told me." I can tell he's mentally checking off all those times I've dropped the ball on my parental responsibilities: pickups, driving to tournaments out of town, taking the kids to visit my ailing father.

"It's not just mono." I can feel tears welling up behind my eyes. "I'm sick."

"What's wrong? What is it?" He's thinking the worst. "Cancer?"

"No. Nothing like that. Nothing physical." I stumble toward an explanation. "My anxiety has got really bad. I can't work, I can't drive, I can barely be alone in my own house."

"Sorry. I didn't know." He looks intently at his bottle of Kokanee, picks at a corner of the label with his fingernail. "That explains a few things."

"It started five months ago. I couldn't sleep. It just kept getting worse."

Slowly, carefully, he peels off the label.

"I went through that right after we split up," he says. "The not-sleeping part. Worrying about everything."

"I never knew that. Sorry."

"Well, I got through it. That's when I started running. It helped." He looks up at me. "Have you tried running?"

I think of my twice-daily walks, my nightly journalling, my desperate prayers, my thirteen doctors.

"I've tried everything. I'm on antidepressants."

He looks stricken, shocked, then catches himself. "Are they helping?"

"A little. I think. I'm not really sure. Is there anything I can do to help?"

On that warm Saturday afternoon, we finally laid down our weapons—the words that had kept us sparring for years—and listened.

△ △ △

I COULDN'T TALK to Kim anymore. She had such high hopes for my healing but as I began to second-guess the New Age thing, she got downright mean. "What makes you think antidepressants will help you feel any better?" or "All you want is a padded room on a psychiatric ward. You aren't strong enough to make a new choice."

My sister Robin, the mean one from our teens, has been surprisingly supportive. She's had some serious health issues herself and had tried the naturopathic route, too. "They all have their blind spots," she said of doctors in general and our older sister in particular. "You have to figure out what is right for you."

I haven't told my mother a thing.

She has enough to worry about, after all. Taking care of Dad, managing her own precarious health and looking after the house and yard on her own.

"How are you feeling?" she asks me at every phone call.

"Fine." My voice sounds thin and pale. "Just overtired."

"Are you sure?" She knows I am lying.

I don't want to cause her any more pain.

This is a new memory.

It springs up unbidden, too bright and too fast, like a Super 8 home movie, jumping and chattering in a darkened basement.

My mother is vacuuming vigorously in my mint-green and pink bedroom. The vacuum knocks the plastic floor protectors out from beneath the bed legs. Mom hoists the bed frame, nudging them back into place with her foot.

I race into the room—a child of nine or ten—and flop down on my bed.

The bedpost crushes the top of my mother's foot.

I hear her yelp of pain, see tears squeeze through scrunched-up eyes.

I'm sorry. I'm sorry. I'm sorry.

She says it was an accident. She knows I didn't do it on purpose. Later, she shows me the bruises on her foot, purple and swollen, under a tea-towel filled with ice.

I go to my bedroom and close the door quietly. I pile a stack of *Reader's Digest Condensed* books on the bed. I throw on my Companion Library hardcovers: *Black Beauty* and *Call of the Wild, Treasure Island* and *Kidnapped,* and all my beloved Nancy Drews.

I lift the bed frame, slide my bare foot beneath and let go.

△ △ △

IT IS MOTHER'S DAY. Day thirty-two for medication. Celexa each morning. Ativan as required. Zopiclone at bedtime.

I wake up after another restless night to fresh flowers and a card perched on my bedside table.

"To Mom. Hope you feel better soon. Love Robert and Michael."

I feel a sudden wave of longing I recognize from long ago. I am homesick. I want to see my mom.

Gerald, pulled from his gentle Sunday morning routine, offers to drive me to Calgary. He'll drop me off and run some errands so I can visit on my own.

I am standing in front of my parents' house. Trying to look pulled together even though I have fallen apart.

I walk up the front steps. The Kingsland house is now a fortress. A Bulldog Home Security sign is planted in the front garden where the peonies and columbines used to bloom. I follow the little sidewalk that loops around to the backyard. White metal bars barricade the basement windows. Motion detector lights, tripped by pesky black squirrels and high winds, strobe on and off at dusk. A Neighbourhood Watch decal on the back door warns would-be intruders: *Our toaster and microwave are secretly encrypted.* Even the milk chute is soldered shut.

Stable home begets stable family.

Past the opening pleasantries and the perfunctory kiss, we settle: Mom, Dad and I, in the living room on the recently reupholstered chesterfield and chairs. There is the usual question about the drive down and wasn't it a lovely day for it?

Yes. Lovely. (I wish to God I could drive on my own.)

"Would you like some tea?" Mom asks. "I can throw on the kettle." She walks into the kitchen with an off-rhythm side-to-side gait, like a metronome out of kilter.

For a while, it is just my dad and me in silence. He is even more withdrawn and frail. Depressed, say the doctors. Maybe he's just tired and bored, like that angel sitting on a cloud in a *Far Side* cartoon thinking: "Wish I'd brought a magazine."

I try to come up with a startling fact or news item to discuss. There hasn't been a recent plane crash or natural disaster we can chat about. Neither of us has the energy for the dinosaur debate anymore.

"How are the kids?" Dad asks finally.

"Good, really good," I say, seizing the invitation. "Their sports keep us pretty busy."

He nods. Smiles slightly.

Uninteresting.

"Robert just got his driver's licence."

"He did, did he?"

Was that a spark of interest?

"I told him Granddad could probably give him a couple pointers on driving a standard shift."

He nods. Smiles slightly. He hasn't driven for over a year.

Fizzle.

"Tea's ready," Mom calls out.

Dad shuffles back to bed. He's wearing slippers and the blue jacquard bathrobe we bought him for Father's Day thirty years ago. I've never seen him wear it. This will be the last memory I have of him in this house.

"Thanks for the visit," he says, ever courteous, before closing his bedroom door.

I walk into the kitchen. Sit at the head of the table where Dad used to.

Mom sets the old Peak Frean cookie tin in front of me, tugs at the lid. "Would you like a jam-jam?"

"Sure."

She touches my hair, then strokes my sleeve.

"How are you feeling?" she asks. "Honestly."

There are layers of surface on these kitchen walls. Dark wood covers brick-patterned wallpaper. Beneath that, the walls are painted an unforgettable celery green.

I want to pry up a panel board section, peel the wallpaper down to the paint. Back to the time when I could tell my mother everything and she would say all the right things to make things all right.

How can I possibly tell her about this?

Honestly, Mom? I have GAD.

No, sounds too much like STD.

Honestly, Mom? I have a generalized anxiety disorder, which has led to a clinical depression.

No, too DSM-IV-ish.

Honestly, Mom? I'm on drugs.

No. What if she blames herself? What if she makes me move back home?

I take a deep breath.

"Honestly, Mom? I've been having a really hard time."

She sits beside me. Silently. She does not rush in with "oh dear" or "poor thing."

The rest of my words spill out in a gut-wrenching rant.

"I feel like I've failed at everything."

◊ ◊ ◊

AS MY SOBS SUBSIDE, I hear the steady hum of the fridge. Birds chirping in the backyard. The distant drone of a lawn mower.

"More tea?" Mom asks. Everything seems fine after a good cup of tea.

She pours and sits down again. She curls her fingers and surveys her nails. An old habit.

Smiling faces stare back at me from the dining room wall. A huge family photo portrait taken in 1987. A moment caught before everything changed.

My parents with sound limbs, strong hearts and unclouded eyes smile at the photographer, who leaps on long legs in black leather pants between camera and family tableau. He arranges the three daughters around Mother in the chair. Stand. Kneel. Sit. Father stands solidly in the background—much like he did in real life. There are no accidents or divorces or illnesses that will jolt each of us out of lives we believed, in this picture anyway, we had perfectly under control.

Mom takes a sip of tea. "Do you remember when your dad had his difficult time? When he couldn't eat or sleep and began to do all sorts of strange things?"

I nod. "Like pulling all the wiring out of the basement?"

"Remember when he finally had to be admitted to the hospital?"

"Yeah. Robert played checkers with him there."

"I visited your dad every day. We went for short walks and played shuffleboard and Scrabble—and you know how your dad dislikes games. Some weekends, he was allowed to come home."

I remember. Our shadow father sitting in his favourite chair, searching for signs of his solid, reliable self.

"Your dad was in hospital for over a month. His psychiatrist—such a good man—was worried about how I was holding up under the strain. I told him I was fine, of course."

Of course she would.

"One afternoon, I came home from the hospital. Your sister Robin was here for a visit. We were having tea at the table just like we are now. And I started to cry—which you know I never do in front of you girls—and I couldn't stop. I just sat there sobbing. I felt so stupid. Robin told me that it was all right to cry, that I had been through a rough time. She said, 'It's okay to ask for help.'"

This image of my sister being kind to Mom lingers.

"So the next day, after morning Mass, I went to see the doctor. I told him how I was *really* feeling. Angry, sad, worried. He prescribed something to help me."

"Epsom salts?"

"No, thank God." She laughs. "Something with an *x* in it."

She covers my hand with hers, serious again.

"You will get through this. You haven't failed at all."

I stare at the blue-veined, sinewy hand over mine.

"Trust your doctor and trust the medication. Trust yourself."

She squeezes my hand and lets go.

My mother has released me.

Trust yourself.

◇ ◇ ◇

MY DAD DIED later that May. He spent his final weeks at the same nursing home where, just a few years earlier, he'd played his saxophone for the weekly seniors' dances. On Friday of the Victoria Day weekend, he got the stomach flu. By Sunday, he was having seizures. Paramedics took him to Rockyview, where the nurses monitored his pain and kept him comfortable. Dad died early Monday morning. My mother and sister arrived just minutes after he'd gone. That's the way he would have wanted it. No bother to any-one. No funeral or fanfare. He had decided decades earlier to donate his body to medical research.

When I think of Dad's quiet passing, I imagine him step-ping into that single yellow tile in the floor of his downstairs office and going back to Whitewood, Saskatchewan. He is greeted by his mother and father, sister Agnes and brother Roly, together once again in their "Bide-a-Wee" summer cottage at Round Lake. There will be a dance at the hall tonight. Agnes will play the piano, George will play the sax-ophone and Roly will dance with the girls. Just like all those Victoria Day weekends years ago.

Play on, Dad.

◊ ◊ ◊

I NEVER SAW my dad in the hours before he died, but I did make a decision. Something in his honour, sort of, something that affirmed the faith he had in science and progress and basic human decency. And the faith, however under-communicated, that he'd maybe had in me all along.

Everyone is quiet in this waiting room. We leaf through magazines, read public health posters on the wall or stare at nothing in particular on a nondescript carpet. We avoid eye contact. The receptionist speaks softly, discreetly, behind a counter shielded with Plexiglas. The only other sounds come from a radio tuned into an easy-listening station and the rhythmic tick of the clock on the wall.

This is my first visit to a psychiatrist.

I have not dressed up or rehearsed my lines. I'm feeling a little tense, a little curious, but mostly relieved. One dozen doctors later, I am now ready to see the most dramatized, dreaded doctor of all. (I watched *Desperate Housewives* for the first time last week. Bree, the red-haired, porcelain-skinned one, admits herself to a psychiatric hospital. The sinister male psychiatrist tries to give her drugs that will make her dull, compliant and plain. Desperate, she tries to escape.)

The doctor steps out of her office and invites me in.

She is younger than me. And beautiful. More *Vogue* than *Psychiatric Times*.

She motions to the chairs opposite a huge expanse of oak desk. No black leather couch in sight.

"How can I help you?"

I tell her about the past six months, weaving in my anxious proclivities of the past forty-odd years. "My mother fell on me when she was six months pregnant. Maybe I had anxiety *in utero*." I can't resist throwing that in.

She smiles a little, taking notes in large, looping letters.

"It sounds like you know yourself pretty well."

I tell her I have spent the better part of twenty years dodging the antidepressant bullet. Until lately.

"That's normal," she assures me. "No one likes to take medication. Especially anxious people. But anxiety never really goes away completely."

I tell her that I've always found ways to cope. Talk therapy. Writing. Walking. Why aren't those working anymore?

"Well, research shows that when women are into their forties, the things we coped with before can become overwhelming. Cumulative stress from work and family. Aging parents. Perimenopause…"

I tell her I have been taking an antidepressant for eight weeks, three days and five hours.

"Are you feeling better?"

That's a tricky question. Like an optometrist asking, "Which is better? A or B? Better or worse?" as he clicks through lenses in a darkened room.

Some things are better. My appetite is back. I've stopped losing weight. I can concentrate enough to read a book or watch a movie. I'm not obsessing about going crazy or being left alone with the knives. But I still can't drive highways or stay alone in my house for very long. Those anxious sensations won't go away. The shortness of breath, burning throat, stomach pains.

"Have you had those checked out?"

Yes. Respiratory test. Gallbladder ultrasound. Upper GI tract X-ray. All normal.

She scrawls "GAD" on the bottom of the page.

"Your physical symptoms are typical of a generalized anxiety disorder," she says, making notes. "The antidepressant has helped a little, but I want to prescribe something that works directly on the anxiety. A benzodiazepine. Long-acting. Very effective."

She stops writing and looks up at me. I must look skeptical, maybe scared.

"Imagine you have a wound here," she says, demonstrating on her own wrist. "This is something we can apply directly to heal it."

I watch her fingertips smooth over the veins on the inside of her wrist, gently, tenderly. A gesture of infinite care.

She peels a sheet from her prescription pad and gives it to me.

"This will help you get your life back."

Her words are like water.

△ △ △

THAT NIGHT I fall gently asleep. Next night, same thing. And the night after that.

The anxiety has released me.

For now.

Forever?

I don't know.

But for now, it is enough.

FORTY-FIVE YEARS AFTER I was born, I left the womb for good.

I lie on the thick green grass where my snow angels have melted away. I look up at an indigo night sky and imagine this:

There is a cord that has always connected my mother and me: invisible but strong. Maybe it is a bluish-grey umbilical cord or maybe a child's hot-pink skipping rope. I cut the imaginary cord with big silver shears. I bury it beneath my towering Arbour Day spruce tree in our Kingsland backyard.

My mother no longer needs to protect me. She has given me enough.

I no longer need to protect her. I have been good enough.

The road continues richly, suspensefully, beyond the edge of a loose-leaf map.

I am not afraid.

Christmas morning.
Does it get any better than this?

Christmas afternoon. Everyone needs a nap.

(My mother sewed these smocks from scritchy-
scratchy fabric. Note that I have only two treble clefs
stitched in festive red ric-rac. Mom must have run out
of time—or ric-rac. As a child I resented this.
As an adult I totally get it.)

DEC

63

My new Chatty Cathy doll. Golden hair, blue eyes and a
voice. "Will you play with me?" "Let's change my dress."
"May I have a cookie?" "Tell me a story." After a while, I
quit pulling her cord and made up my own lines.

The Campbell girls: Kim, Robin and Miji. My mother still
introduces me as "Daughter number three."

This unintentional double exposure is haunting. There
are so few pictures of Dad. Here, he is both contented father
and solitary musician, playing his saxophone.

Family summer holidays. Seven sun-filled days at
the Wagon Wheel Motel in Radium, BC. New friends
to keep us afloat in the pools at Fairmont and
Radium Hot Springs.

First-day-of-school ritual. Mom takes our photo
in front of the weeping birch. Years later, her six
grandsons would climb that tree.

This is one of the few photos of the whole family together,
including Haggis the dog.

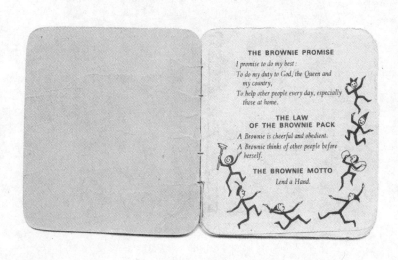

THE BROWNIE PROMISE

I promise to do my best:
To do my duty to God, the Queen and
my country,
To help other people every day, especially
those at home.

THE LAW
OF THE BROWNIE PACK

A Brownie is cheerful and obedient.
A Brownie thinks of other people before
herself.

THE BROWNIE MOTTO

Lend a Hand.

The Brownie rules left little room for having a bad day.

The Catholic rules at least had Confession.

My only keepsake of Woodward's: an empty box.
Seeing it still makes me wistful.

My Midge doll. She may have been Barbie's
best friend, but she was nowhere near as glamorous.
Even in her velvet and taffeta ball gown.

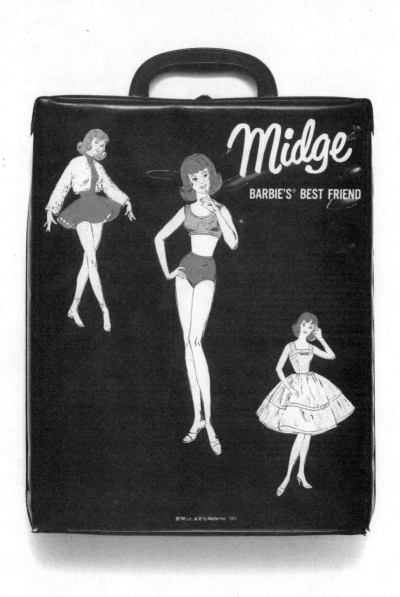

And this is where Midge lived.
(Note the wholesome girl-next-door vibe.)

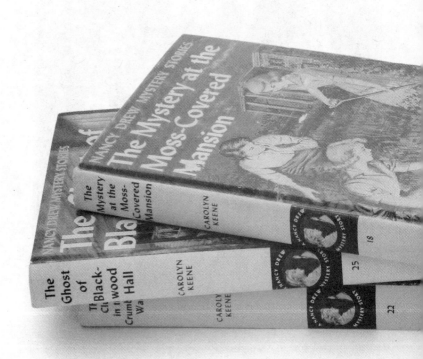

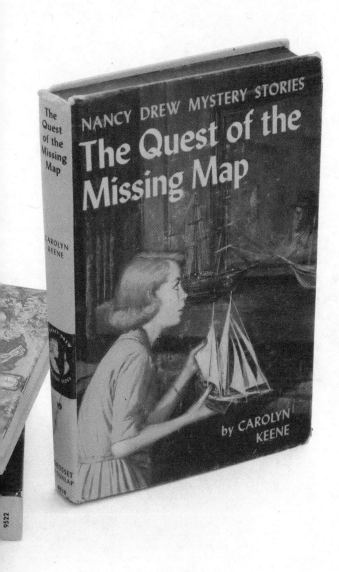

My first Nancy Drew mystery.
The cover illustration scared me to death.

My childhood touchstones of romance to come.

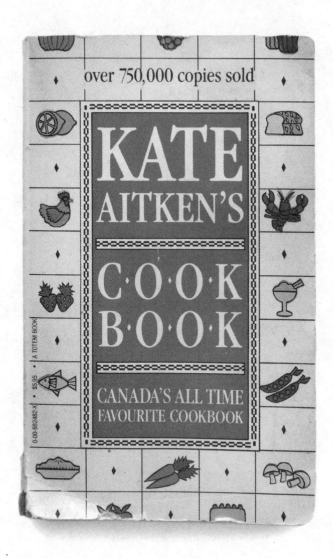

over 750,000 copies sold

KATE AITKEN'S

C·O·O·K B·O·O·K

CANADA'S ALL TIME FAVOURITE COOKBOOK

A TOTEM BOOK • $5.95 • 0-00-692482-X

I knew there would be cooking involved.

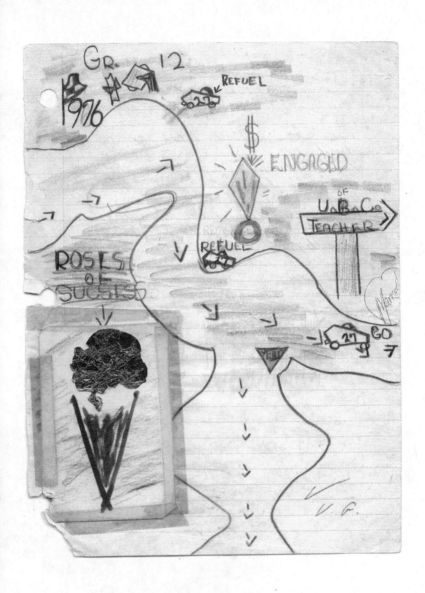

Is the path ever more certain
and clear as when you are ten?

MAGIC *Etch A Sketch* ® SCREEN

Shake, forgive and begin again.

{ ACKKNOWLEDGEMENTS }

DESPITE MY EARLIER AVERSION to lists, I have come to appreciate their value. My thanks to:

1. Jesse Finkelstein of Page Two Strategies, who believed in the power of an ordinary story. For her expert guidance and unwavering vision.

2. Jennifer Griffiths, for her brilliant cover art and book design.

3. Michelle MacAleese, copyeditor, and Judy Phillips, proofreader. They left no phrase unturned.

4. Charlotte Gill, Betsy Warland, Daphne Read and Greg Hollingshead, who read my early drafts, discerning a hopeful shape in a heap of story fragments.

5. Marni Jackson, whose words inspired me to write in the first place.

6. My sister Kim, who listened and laughed in just the right places over long-distance phone lines.

7. My sister Robin. She didn't like me tagging along as a kid but she's walked beside me, steady and sure, on this journey.

8. My sons, who have grown into young men with kind, brave hearts. I hope this book captures our story, since I never finished their baby books.

9. My husband, Gerald, who supported me in every way imaginable. "Dreams first, mortgage later."

10. My mom, dad and our Kingsland.

MIJI CAMPBELL is a writer and teacher. Her work has appeared in numerous publications, including *Today's Parent*, *The Edmonton Journal*, *The Calgary Herald* and *Women's Words: An Anthology*, and has been broadcast on CBC Radio. Miji has received two National Magazine Award nominations and a literary arts grant from the Alberta Foundation for the Arts. She owns *Write Where You Are*, a business that offers writing workshops to individuals, schools and community and corporate organizations. Born and raised in Calgary, Miji lives in Red Deer, Alberta. *Separation Anxiety* is her first book.